AMERICAN STYLE

METROPOLITAN HOME

AMERICAN STYLE

DYLAN LANDIS

 CLARKSON POTTER/PUBLISHERS NEW YORK

Published by Clarkson N. Potter, Inc., 201 East 50th
Street, New York, New York 10022. Member of the
Crown Publishing Group.

Random House, Inc. New York, Toronto, London,
Sydney, Auckland

www.randomhouse.com

CLARKSON N. POTTER, POTTER, and colophon are
registered trademarks of Random House, Inc.

Printed in China

Design by Richard Ferretti

Library of Congress Cataloging-in-Publication Data
Landis, Dylan, 1956–
    American style / by Dylan Landis. — 1st ed.
    Includes bibliographical references and index.
    1. Interior decoration—United States—History—
20th century. I. Title.
NK2004.L36   1999
747.213—dc21   98-41867

ISBN 0-517-70761-6

10 9 8 7 6 5 4 3 2 1

First Edition

FOREWORD

Since the late 1960s, when *Metropolitan Home®* was founded (as *Apartment Life*), the editors of the magazine have tracked a sea change in residential style. This shift in domestic design has been as significant in our field as the American Revolution was to our nation's political consciousness in the eighteenth century.

How we choose to shape the architecture of our homes and what we choose to put in them say as much about who we are these days as how we vote and what we do at work. Vernacular styles are far from dead, but homes now reflect inner personal geography as much as the topography of the neighboring landscape. We are no longer content to inherit our parents' or grandparents' ideas about style (although many of us cherish and incorporate them). And even when we employ professional designers, we insist on full participation and line-item veto power. We've rejected the match-and-match design philosophy of earlier decades, preferring to relish the fun, the freedom, and the individuality of mixing. We have an enduring respect for our various regional architectures, but we see no reason why a New England saltbox can't happily house a collection of Senegalese tribal masks.

And if we no longer like slavish imitation or period copies, we certainly tend to take style less seriously than in days gone by, so we display a healthy dose of humor (and often irreverence). Creativity, quirk, innovation, history, and heart meet in many of the homes in these pages. Even a partial list of the "period styles" from which people now routinely sample shows the freewheeling invention we've brought home, from Greek Revival and Italian Renaissance to Arts and Crafts and Art Deco all the way up to the postmodern, deconstructionist, and minimalist modes. We think a Bauhaus-inspired home *can* easily accommodate choice American antiques. A converted barn's shingled exterior may give no hint of the sybaritic tiled bath within. Not to mention styles that defy conventional nomenclature, like Pacific Rim meets Hollywood Glamour or neoclassic French country meets Miami modern with a Caribbean twist.

Combined with a strong sense of place, this sure sense of self makes American style sophisticated yet comfortably intimate—and what better way to live as we begin the 21st century!

Donna Warner
Editor in Chief
METROPOLITAN HOME®

CONTENTS

PRIDE OF PLACE

Most of us have read enough, and moved enough, to know that home feels like *Home* only when it mirrors our private passions—whether for order, for color, for Tuscan villas, or for peace. But a house best reflects its owner's soul when it is faithful to itself as well—when it honors the region around it, nods at the architectural traditions that are its legacy. That's why the best design goes one step beyond, say, merely updating a '70s kitchen, or making the bath sybaritic, or coaxing sunlight into a shaded bedroom.

It's also about restoring a house to its true voice, and remembering where you live.

So if, like antique dealers Jim Hanson and Steve Douthit, you move your lush Victorian furniture into a derelict Minnesota farmhouse and launch a renovation, you also leave unaltered the brick facade, the quiet grace, the 19th-century Midwestern modesty. Paint a checkerboard floor in the parlor, yes—but leave it unsealed to scuff.

If, like architect Tom McCallum, you confront a Seattle-area split-level ranchburger, you might recall the Arts and Crafts bungalows that were its architectural forebears. You renovate evocatively, installing cherry ceilings and windows gridded like a Macintosh chair. Rebuilding the facade, you choose water-smoothed stones from a Washington riverbed.

Or if, like restaurateurs George Germon and Johanne Killeen, you faux-gild the walls of your Rhode Island home, then you also leave intact the plank ceilings and industrial door that announce your real address: a 19-century barge, permanently moored at a working boatyard.

One hand designs. The other, sometimes, restrains. Think homage, not slavish devotion; play up contrasts, not just similarities. Take inspiration from design lessons in other parts of the country—they can often cross state lines, with some creative adaptation.

"It's a very mature approach," says New York designer Mariette Himes Gomez. In Santa Fe, she points out, you might naturally gravitate toward primitive furniture—but not the expected Mexican. "I'd look for something from another culture: Italian or American, or French painted pieces," she says. "Something rustic enough to relate to the area but also different enough to transcend it."

Balance is everything, as the Zen masters say. One ear is tuned to your own desires. The other is cocked for what the land has to say.

In Texas, it might say that a sprawling metal toolshed, so typical of the region's outbuildings, should be taken apart and reconstructed as a house. In New York City, it might suggest that movie-theater carpeting, dancing with pattern (to obscure the Pepsi spills), is ideal for a five-story stair at the core of a narrow townhouse. And in rural Wisconsin, it might humble the newest stewards of a four-room wooden house, built centuries ago by settlers. The owners are fond of things French and Italian, which explains the formal garden, the Louis chairs, a *faux marbre* floor. Yet even with this European accent, the house still tells the story of its lowborn past. No paint has ever touched its walls. Its electrical wiring is minimal (some might say inadequate). And the marble floors are in fact hand-painted floorcloths, a veracious echo of a settler's rug.

This is design honesty, a.k.a. regionally sensitive design. Or, simply, truth in decorating, if that sounds more accessible. It's the subtle principle that invites you to exercise your design fantasies without exorcising your surroundings, or the past.

The people involved with these 39 homes know what it means to listen to a house, to honor the place where it was born. They know what it means to brand each room with their own tastes and artistic leanings, while weaving in at least one element that makes their home truly Texan. Or Californian. Or so unmistakably New York.

The result is harmony—a home that expresses you, as well as your place on this earth; a sense that your rooms, unlike those in chain hotels, could exist no place else except precisely where they are.

The result is pride of place.

CALIFORNIA

WHETHER INFORMED BY THE GLAMOUR OF HOLLYWOOD OR THE DISCRETION OF THE FAR EAST, THESE HOUSES OF THE "NEW" WEST ARE INVESTED WITH A SENSE OF THE PAST

11

BERKELEY MODERN: A COPPER-CLAD PHOENIX

When a fire destroys a house, how does one rebuild—with an eye to the future, or in remembrance of things past? Sharon Drager, a physician who lost her Berkeley home to the devastating 1991 fire, refused to look back. She hired architect Frank Israel, whose buildings are famous for their energy, elegance, and a certain amount of discord, to design a new shelter.

From outside, the house appears to have emerged from a difficult birth—triumphant, intact, but slightly askew. Overhangs are generous with shade, but asymmetrically slanted. Windows are liberal with glass, but twisted into trapezoids. The chimney, clad in copper, leans into the house so deeply it bisects the roof. "The Berkeley spirit of experimentation really enters into this house," says Annie Chu, the project architect and a former partner in Israel Callas Shortridge. "This is a very modern brand of domesticity."

Sharon Drager calls it her phoenix, and finds comfort inside. "Every room takes advantage of the light," she says, "and every room is comfortable in a different way." Israel (who died in 1996) knew his client wanted a sense of communion when she was home with her teenage children, and he found ways to interlock the rooms and views from one floor to the next. Drager's fourth-story bedroom offers an oblique glimpse, as if from an indoor balcony, of the living room one flight down; her third-floor study, with partial walls, lets her monitor comings and goings along the entry hall and stairs. "We took a traditional study, blew the walls out, and put it in a position of power," says Chu. "Almost all the public spaces let you overlook, or at least sense, what's going on elsewhere in the house."

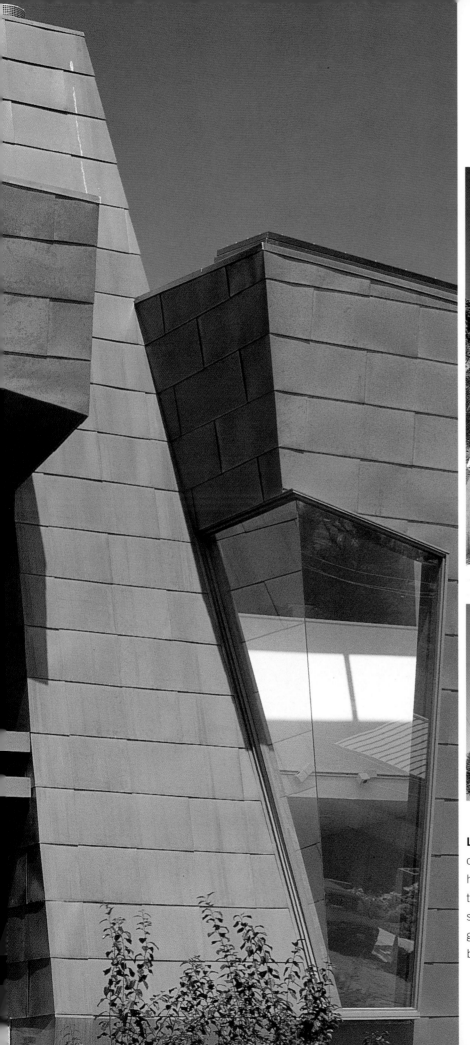

Left: The chimney, cloaked in the same fire-resistant copper shingles as the roof, presses into the side of the house as if pinning it to the hillside. **Top:** Like a fortress, the front of the house presents no entry to the street; stairs, at right, lead to a side entrance. **Above:** The glassed-in top floor holds Drager's bedroom suite; just below is her study.

WHAT THE PROS KNOW ABOUT
PIGMENTED PLASTER

When pigment gets stirred into plaster, color becomes integral to the wall. It weathers more gracefully than paint, may endure decades longer, and suffers less damage from minor chips. Not every plasterer can do the job: it takes experience to mix the right color (this aubergine hearth required 24 samples) and strength to repeatedly burnish each coat. "It's twice the work and twice the price of plain plastering," says Israel partner Barbara Callas. Lessons from the firm:

- Blue pigment fades in direct sunlight.
- Too much pigment weakens plaster.
- For high impact and lower cost, save pigmented plaster for one wall or focal point.

Opposite: The fireplace is flanked on both sides by open space. As a result, the hearth wall is not merely domestic, but sculptural. **Left:** Because rooms are terraced down the hill, Israel could carve out tall columns of empty space. The windowed columns serve as light wells and offer partial views from one floor to the next.

At the same time, the house is full of private realms. Instead of bedrooms, Israel created bedroom suites, each with its own bath and dressing room, and made sure that no two suites would face each other across a hall. And to keep Drager's study from becoming common ground, he built a second study for her children.

Drager's bedroom is custom-fitted to her habits: the reading corner includes a fireplace, a chaise, and built-in shelves. The living room, though used formally, has similar cues for intimacy: the plaster on its walls was color-matched to an old aubergine shoe that Drager loves, and its chairs are overscaled, the way an inviting chair appears to a child.

There are no antiques or mementos here; none survived. But young California live oaks are growing outside, replacing grand specimens that burned. A terrace garden is planted in colors that Drager chose. And though the house itself is more invention than tradition, its Arts and Crafts materials—copper, stucco, cedar siding—make it somehow familiar, and at home on the quickening land.

Opposite: Because the dining room doubles as a conference room, Israel placed it near the entryway. The clerestory window, so tall it illuminates both the third and fourth floors, makes the source of light almost celestial. Painting by Pamela Smilow. **Above left:** The desk and walls of Drager's study, paneled in Finnish birch plywood, read as a single piece of cabinetry that frames the trapezoidal window. Puzzle chair by local designer David Kawecki. **Left:** The bedroom hearth follows the exterior, angular form of the chimney. Interior designers Karen Ross and Wendy Bunch, who helped Drager refurnish after the fire, defined a reading corner with the Donghia chaise. **Above:** Nearly every doorway frames a view of the three-story staircase, whose walls are sometimes canted, sometimes straight.

MISSION STYLE, REIGNITED BY ROMANCE

From its circular foyer to a living room that resembles a small church, this 1930s Los Angeles house had all the architectural graces of the Spanish Colonial style. It also had chalk-white walls—until film director Brian Gibson hired designer Michael Anderson.

Anderson's first move was structural: he replaced expanses of plate glass, installed in the 1950s, with vintage-look French windows and doors. Bound by a budget, however, he knew the real magic would have to be worked with paint. He called on Stephen LeClair, a decorative artist, and together they ragged, dragged, and combed the walls with saffron-colored glazes. For ceilings, they mixed stormy blues and grays; on woodwork, they switched to leathery reds. As the layered glazes grew vibrant, along came men bearing sandpaper to erode the newness. "These finishes are expressive and aged."

Unspoken rules establish order. Spicy colors are banded by darker or cooler hues, for example, offering visual relief. Yellow is so widely used that it has settled into the role of an undemanding neutral. And all the patterns, however exotic, are based on a folk art tradition. Says Anderson, "These finishes aren't faux anything."

Left: Anderson replicated the effects of a relentless sun by painting the terrace's stucco arches blue—then sandblasting. **Right:** Anderson's painting of a primitive Christ child transforms a flat wooden '50s door. The blue tile border is a figment of paint: before the glaze dried, the designer wrapped his fingertip in a rag, dipped it in paint thinner, and drew grout lines every few inches.

WHAT THE PROS KNOW ABOUT
DECORATIVE PAINTING

Walls rubbed with saffron paint can look glorious in a Mediterranean-style house, but in a less theatrical ranch house or white-box apartment, decorative painting thrives on subtlety. To gently age Sheetrock walls so they appear to have been washed with tea, Neil Janovic, vice president of Janovic/Plaza Decorating Centers, recommends a paint-store product called French Wash One-Step Sponging Paint, in Blush. Lay on a cream-colored latex base coat, then apply the wash with a small-pored natural sponge (tiny pores create a lacier, less sponged-on look) or a rag. (Experiment first on paper with various strokes: pouncing, rubbing, ragging.) If desired, sand lightly in spots when the wash dries, allowing the base coat to glow through. Small rooms, particularly foyers and baths, can contain bolder finishes, like marbleized moldings in an entry hall. Designer Vicente Wolf's shortcut: wad up a banner of Saran Wrap, dip very lightly into paint, and touch it to the woodwork; the crinkles create the veining. "In small doses," says New York designer Christopher Coleman, "you can exercise any fantasy."

Opposite: The study's wainscoting and chair rail are glazed on the wall. Brian Gibson, the homeowner, adopted the green chair for its rusticity, though its height makes it inhospitable. **Above:** Curried colors in the breakfast room are balanced by celadon ceramics and blue-gray beams. **Below:** As if illuminating an altar, Anderson punched a Spanish quatrefoil window high into the living room; the painted starburst around it was adapted from a New Mexico church.

THE ELEGANCE OF A WELL-EDITED SPACE

When Peter Carlson married Linda Chase, they needed not only a home, but a common ground for the furnishings they had amassed separately for years. His antiques tend to be stately, like Empire chairs whose gilded arms are carved in the shape of swans. Hers have a regal delicacy: a Louis XVI bed, for example, with fluted, tapering legs. And together they collected modern pieces, which explains the startling sight of two wiry Bertoia chairs.

Carlson and Chase are both interior designers, and they were drawn to a Spanish Colonial cottage in the Hollywood Hills with pleasingly quirky features—a niche in the hall, a sunken living room, graceful curvature where the ceilings meet the walls. To cleanse the backdrop for their disparate collections, the couple "painted out the interior," as Carlson puts it, applying linen-white paint to every surface of the house and even rubbing it, slightly thinned, into the floorboards. (Polyurethane adds the sheen.) "We wanted to be able to read the wood," says Carlson, "but lose the golden-oak tone." Plate-glass windows, a previous owner's 1960s addition, were replaced with banks of French windows and doors; daylight now washes the textured plaster walls, and sets the floors aglow.

Rigorous editing and styling set up a kinship between furnishings of different periods. Tones of mahogany and gold dominate the mix, and even the chromed-steel Bertoia chairs are upholstered in pale gold Fortuny fabric. "When proportions are compatible and one palette ties everything together," says Chase, "it's always more interesting to marry a lot of styles."

Above: In the living room, seating tends to be relaxed, like the Lawson-style armchair upholstered in cut velvet. With the comfort level high, Carlson and Chase can indulge in more courtly pieces—an American Empire console, at left, and the pair of Sèvres urns on the mantel. **Far left:** Coaxing Fortuny fabric around the wide curves of the 1952 chromed-steel chair by Harry Bertoia "nearly drove our upholsterer mad," says Carlson. **Left:** A 1930s straw marquetry screen by Jean-Michel Frank makes an angular foil for a Louis XVI chair.

Left: Carlson aligned 18th- and 19th-century drawings and watercolors with the tops of door frames—a simple way of organizing even a disparate collection of framed art. **Above:** Pictures in the hallway, tightly packed, climb straight to the slender crown molding. **Right:** The plain gilt frame of the bedroom's 19th-century Swedish mirror defers to a painted Italian chest of drawers.

WHAT THE PROS KNOW ABOUT
ARRANGING ARTWORK

Linda Chase hangs pictures largely by eye; Peter Carlson works out the coordinates of every nail. But both designers begin the same way—on the floor, not the wall. They favor a rectangular arrangement whose structure, or layout, is almost architectural. "Anchor the corners first," advises Carlson. He particularly likes splitting up pairs of pictures to balance the top or bottom corners; if no pairs are available, he suggests using images with dark mats, which carry more weight than white ones. Next, focus on the middle (not necessarily dead center), giving the eye a place to land. "Something small with a very wide mat will draw you in," says Carlson. "So will one large picture, or two or three related pieces." The designers stir in watercolors, drawings, and prints that share either bright or muted tones. (Oil paintings should hang alone or with each other, however; in a mixed grouping, they would steal the show.) Don't bother striving for a perfect grid, the designers advise; once the perimeter is straight, the remaining frames don't have to align. To hang, transfer the perimeter measurements to the wall so the center of the grouping is at eye level or slightly above. A strip of Scotch tape, applied before hammering and left in place, helps keep plaster walls from cracking.

NEW HOLLYWOOD MODERN: GLAMOUR AND WIT

This 1930s Monterrey Colonial was sold as a teardown, valued only for its upper-crust Brentwood location. But Peter Benedek, a talent and literary agent, and his screenwriter wife, Barbara, were charmed by its pretensions. A diamond-paned bay window adorned its brick-and-wood facade; so did Regency-swagged iron railings. "It looked like a mansion in three-quarter scale," says Roy McMakin, the Los Angeles designer who gave the house two additions, three terraces and porches, and custom furniture throughout. "And it seemed to be a great foil for the plainness of my work."

The living room, original to the house, is an architecturally dressy space. Moldings panel the walls in a *rinceau* treatment, and the neoclassical hearth invites a formal seating arrangement. "This isn't a movie-star house, but it plays off that Hollywood sensibility," says McMakin. "The living room needed something sensual." He designed twin sofas with Mae West curves to the back and arms, and more than a hint of languor. They are sheathed in smoky green satin, with matching pillows that suggest plump buttons, and they preen near a pair of black side chairs whose legs evoke a woman's calf.

McMakin also designed two rear wings, doubling the square footage of the house and

Right: Treating the house as an underscaled estate, McMakin overscaled the porch furniture. His table, side chairs, and rockers are each painted a slightly different shade of yellow.

Above: Distilling a table to its essence, McMakin comes up with elemental forms like those in the Benedeks' living room. The oval sheet of glass on a rectangular coffee table is his witty way of nudging a plain piece of furniture toward elegance. **Left:** McMakin gave the kitchen its gridlike arrangement of cabinetry, and its subtle detailing —like cutouts instead of knobs. Note the tea-rose cutout in the recessed cabinet at right, and the curl of smoke in the one across the room. **Opposite:** Side chairs, with their swayback forms, practically flirt with the stocky table. The Waterford chandelier, however, strikes a completely different note; McMakin loves quirky contrast and urged the Benedeks to buy it.

significantly raising its luxury quotient. One wing holds a family room with wall-to-wall glass, and, upstairs, an 800-square-foot bath, where the brickwork is pierced with openings as if the tub were not fully indoors. The other wing contains the kitchen, breakfast terrace, second-story terrace, and a gym. Phalanxes of French doors expose both wings to sunlight. "When I'm indoors, I feel as if I'm out," says Peter Benedek. "On weekends, we almost never leave home."

Furnishings for the new rooms bear McMakin's signature right angles and evocative blocky forms. Their proportions stir the memory: a bureau or a chair, stripped of detailing until only the archetype remains, conveys the same simple warmth as something from a childhood bedroom. Contemporary and reassuringly chunky, his furniture gives the Benedeks' new rooms their instant aura of home.

WHAT THE PROS KNOW ABOUT
TOUCHES OF BLACK

Green satin sofas make the Benedeks' living room lush —but black fabric on the side chairs adds the defining edge. "Black has a sophistication that's needed in this charming home," says designer Roy McMakin. "It also lets you focus on the chairs' form and style." There are scores of ways to style a room with notes of black, says Barbara Southerland, an interior designer in Greenville, North Carolina, and New York City. Among her favorites:

■ Bind a sea-grass rug with black canvas edging.

■ Hang a wrought-iron chandelier in the foyer.

■ Install a black Regency chair for instant elegance.

■ Anchor the living room with a square, ebony-stained coffee table.

But know when to stop. "A little black adds punctuation," says Southerland. "Too much loses its punch."

Opposite: Lacy brickwork in the windows of the new master bath invites breezes and dappled sunlight inside, but shields the bathers from view. The glass shutters, also by McMakin, function as windows to keep out the rain. **Above and right:** McMakin created the Benedeks' storage-intensive bed; its headboard shelf is supplemented by recessed compartments in the sides. He also designed the brace of armchairs beneath a David Hockney painting. **Top right:** The dressing-room niche, its oval window, and the Shakeresque bureau beneath it were all designed in concert.

THE TOUCH OF THE FAR EAST

San Francisco has long been a port of entry for goods from the Orient, and the downtown apartment of the late Sandra Sakata, owner of the Sutter Street design boutique Obiko, kept to that exotic tradition. Through her travels she not only stocked Obiko, but wove the fabrics and furnishings of many Asian cultures through her gracious, high-ceilinged rooms.

Her two-bedroom apartment in a 1918 building had the advantage of solid, prewar architecture, including a monumental living-room window that rose straight to the crown molding and opened out, via French doors, to the streetscape. Her furnishings reflected a love of the artisan's touch—in fine Laotian silk ikat fabrics, in Khmer textiles, and in a collection of Silk Route rugs that covered the floor like large stepping-stones and spilled over the sofas as well. For all the pattern at play, however, a sense of balance reigned. Sakata edited her tabletops as if she had just picked up after a tea ceremony, leaving a few well-chosen bowls behind with exquisite restraint. With no wallpaper or curtains to distract the eye, her hand-crafted objects, many from Asian antique shops and flea markets, held the stage. It was not just a design decision, but an act of love: "Behind each piece there's a person," Sakata said. "When I come home, they feel like family."

Left: In Obiko, Sandra Sakata's design shop, jackets made by Janet Kaneko from antique kimonos hang near a Japanese *tansu,* candleholder, and painted screen.

Above: The English Regency-style bamboo tables and cabinets in Sakata's living room are both polished and scarred by age. Japanese lacquerware adds burning shots of color, and Persian rugs are mixed and married according to their spirit, not their provenance. **Left:** A towering Japanese *hinoki* chest-on-chest rules over the living room like an altar, providing a focal point much like a Western-style hearth—and offering boundless storage. The rocker is Appalachian, the rugs Afghani and Persian.

BORROWING LIGHT FROM THE OCEAN AND SKY

Certain times of year, designer Michael Smith stands on the terrace of his Santa Monica apartment and marvels at an ocean that looks frozen and pale. To capture that view, Smith could have mirrored the wall behind his living-room sofa; instead, he stood a silver-leafed screen there. "It has the same quality as the light reflected off the ocean," Smith says. "And it works like a contemporary painting."

California beach homes are often governed by neutral palettes, in deference to water, sand, and sky. Smith prefers a room full of nuance that gradually unfolds. In his contemporary flat, furnishings mingle like guests at a European salon: he styled his sofas after Turkish banquettes, borrowed Japanese form and proportions for his silver screen, and set both against an intricate Agra rug from India. "It feels modern and historical at the same time," he says. "There's tension between the objects, which makes the room more interesting." To that end, a Parsons table—leggy and clean-lined—lands in an arranged marriage with the exotic banquette, while a molded-plywood Eames chair matches curves with a neoclassical fauteuil. Intuition, not tradition, presides over the mix. "I pair elements not for their provenance, but for shape and color and texture," says Smith. "That's when you end up with something very personal."

Right: White walls in the living room reflect sunlight, and focus attention on nearly bare windows. In a typical use of his decorating budget, Michael Smith invested in fabric—here, a striped silk with a sheen for his sofa—but bought the inexpensive pressed-tin table at an import store.

WHAT THE PROS KNOW ABOUT
THE PERFECT COFFEE TABLE

Many people buy elephantine coffee tables, as if equating size with hospitality, notes Michael Smith. But, he cautions, "it throws the room out of scale." Conversely, a meager table leaves visitors holding drinks. Michael Buchanan, a designer with Goralnick ★ Buchanan in New York, reports that certain shapes and sizes succeed almost everywhere—like a 36-inch square, which serves every chair near the sofa. In a small room, choose a table that looks delicate, perhaps lacy wrought-iron under glass. Or pair two smaller squares; they'll suggest cigarette tables and take up less visual space. The standard 18-inch height works because it's roughly level with the sofa seat; for meals, try a 22-inch-high table. Don't cut down an antique dining table, Buchanan warns, as it may emerge clunky; instead, top a piece of architectural salvage with beveled glass.

Opposite: A Georgian writing table makes a dual-purpose, if unorthodox, side table for the sofa. Smith designed a sheathlike slipcover with dressmaker buttons for the 1940s chair. **Above left:** Miniblinds in the living room cut glare. Curtains were banished, as their function would be purely decorative. Sisal flooring and a 1940s cork table add texture without challenging the oceanic blues and greens of the fabrics (and the view). **Above:** In a small study, Smith indulged a taste for orange. Ignoring the usual rule of saving strong colors for accents, he painted walls and ceiling persimmon—making the room so distinct that it seems like a separate "wing."

A HOUSE UNFOLDING AT A GARDEN'S EDGE

Gardens for the great châteaux in France were sometimes seeded years before the house was even built. John Marsh Davis, a Bay Area architect, brought the same reverence to an acre of land he bought in Marin County. He erected a tiny cabin, then spent the next five years working on the hedges, trees, flower beds, and terraced lawns that would define his outdoor rooms. Only time, as Davis points out, can create a timeless garden.

Instead of finally building a house for himself, however, he sold the property, and built one for his buyers instead. The home he designed for David Sheff, an author, and Karen Barbour, an artist, serves a family with children and dogs while honoring the garden's lush formality. It looks, in fact, like a chain of four gazebos, as if the grounds were a grand estate; strung close to the sidewalk, the gazebos – each a room unto itself—make no inroads on the landscaping.

The house adds up to 2,650 square feet, but was designed with intimacy in mind. Its main room—a kitchen, living room, and dining area combined—draws the family together in a single, open chamber. Davis endowed the architecture with a modest magnificence: the mantel over the Rumford fireplace (a high, shallow firebox designed for good heat distribution)

Left: The largest pavilion, at left, is the master bedroom; the second largest, third from left, is the main living room and kitchen. The others contain bedrooms. **Right:** The garden's tiers, seen from a deck outside the main room, step up to a freestanding art studio.

stands higher than 8 feet. French doors and windows are 10 feet tall, and the timber-and-glass ceiling soars to 22 feet. Redwood, a staple of contemporary California houses, is treated with the fine, almost intricate workmanship of the Arts and Crafts period, and the serenity of the space is clearly borrowed from the Japanese.

"I wanted this room to feel both cozy and expansive, a dual challenge," says Davis. "There's mystery to it as well, because the garden and the house unfold into each other."

This unfolding takes place not only through glass, but through slices of mirror that magnify the garden and interior views. Two 10-foot-high mirrors flank the fireplace, for example, each at right angles to the hearth, visually doubling the windows along that wall. Because the mirrors rarely capture human reflections and carry no frames, they are surprisingly hard to spot. It is an exquisite bit of architectural trickery: "Between the huge doors and the overscaled mirrors," says Sheff, "people think there's much more going on in this simple room."

Left: French doors have the proportions of shoji screens. A floor of concrete, evoking the outdoors, links the main room to the wooden deck and the lawns just beyond. Low boxwood hedges cordon off sections of the garden; Italian cypresses add drama and height, expanding the garden vertically. **Below:** The gridlike framework of the fir ceiling marches across an 8-by-14-foot skylight.
Right: Sofas and chairs were chosen for their deep seats and generous size, partly for comfort and partly to pump up the scale of the room.

WHAT THE PROS KNOW ABOUT
RUMFORD FIREPLACES

Many fireplaces are a mixed blessing: much of the air they heat escapes up the chimney, while some of the smoke they produce seeps into the house. But John Davis, like many architects, swears by a 200-year-old aerodynamic design by an inventor named Count Rumford. (Thomas Jefferson was so impressed that he installed several at Monticello.) A Rumford fireplace has noble proportions, as seen in Sheff and Barbour's living room. It is at least as high as it is wide, and shallow, with its side walls angled out so they radiate heat toward the room. Most important, the top of the firebox (the actual fireplace opening) is rounded—a bit of engineering genius that draws a stream of air from the room into the chimney. That air, flowing in, keeps smoke from flowing out. In the 1850s, when Americans started burning coal, the design all but vanished. Now rediscovered, the Rumford comes in kits (except for bricks, which you buy locally). Depending on size, a kit costs about $1,000 from Superior Clay Corporation (800.848.6166 or www.rumford.com).

Left: A seemingly wide window in the main room, at right, is in fact a single, narrow panel that is twinned by its reflection. Just beyond the mirror (more easily identified by its reflection of the mantel) lies the open kitchen, with polished concrete countertops. The floor throughout, of unpolished but sealed concrete, is warmed by a mosaic of rugs.

Opposite: A dining table is loosely set apart from the living area by the back of a sofa. Karen Barbour mixed the kitchen's Giverny-green paint, with subtle differences in hue from one wall to the next. **Far left:** On open shelving above the kitchen sink, neat rows of glasses act as prisms for the sun. **Left:** A bullnose edge refines a concrete work surface. **Below left:** The master bath, with Barbour's artwork, has a concrete-tile, trompe l'oeil floor by San Francisco artisan Buddy Rhodes. **Below:** The master bedroom is larger than the main room, but plainer and constructed with greater economy. "If you have to compromise financially," says Davis, "you put your best foot in the room that you live in."

WITH RESPECT FOR AN EDWARDIAN PAST

In the well-proportioned living room of this 1905 San Francisco town house, prints are hung the old-fashioned way: with brass gallery rods, and a respect for symmetry. Lamp bases shaped like classical urns recall the Grand Tour. A Louis XIV chair, wearing only white muslin, extends equal measures of formality and ease.

But though the details are drawn from the past, they are not in the service of period-pure rooms. "We simply wanted a sense of time, as if someone had lived there forever," says Stephen Brady, vice president of design services for The Limited and a friend of homeowners Patrick Wade and David DeMattei, who invited him to help with the interior. "It looks as if the objects were discovered over decades and had found their place in the room."

Wade, a design consultant, and DeMattei, a retailing executive, gave the house its composure by layering it with hues of cream: vanilla walls, window blinds of eggshell linen, wheat-colored sisal rugs. (Redwood moldings, left dark, provide the necessary architectural definition.) Once this envelope had settled tranquillity on the space, Wade and DeMattei could indulge their eclectic tastes, sending each room on its own stylistic journey without fragmenting the house.

Right: The living room gets its stature from original architectural detail: the fanlight over the window, 18-inch-high baseboards, a prominent redwood hearth. The traditional English-style sofa, chairs, and ottoman are in their summer slipcovers.

Top: In the living room, black opaque lampshades lined with gold paper cast intimate pools of light around the chairs. **Above:** Chunky candles burn in the dining room chandelier; recessed lighting on a dimmer provides backup. Turn-of-the-century photographs of Native Americans are by Edward Curtis. **Right and opposite:** Because the kitchen opens onto the garden, Wade and Brady perceived it as a sunroom. Tactile elements, like a Southwestern rug and the beaded pendant lamp, hint that this is a room for lingering, not just cooking. The leather-topped stools are Brady's design.

Inspired by wood paneling in the dining room, for example, Wade invoked the rough-hewn warmth of the American Southwest. The mesquite table, a prototype he designed for Banana Republic, was handmade in New Mexico with butterfly joints, not nails. Artifacts range from Moroccan pottery to candlesticks from India. "We chose things here for their scale, as we did throughout the house," says Wade. "The point was to have every room feel masculine and welcoming, with a real mix of styles."

The previous owners left the gift of a glassed-in kitchen. Wade's only change was subtle: he gave the white cabinets a coat of lacquer so they would better reflect sunlight from the garden. To the wall of windows he declined to add shades, much as, in the master bedroom, he refrained from draping fabric over a bed frame that seems made for a canopy. "In decorating, one's impulse is usually to add," says Brady. "It's harder, but often wiser, to hold back."

Above: Taking advantage of a fireplace, the master bedroom's architectural extravagance, Brady and Wade angled a pair of deep armchairs with ottomans toward the hearth. Flowers, delivered weekly, are considered a necessary luxury. **Right:** The Shaker-style bed is an ebonized reproduction made in Santa Fe. To honor the volume of empty space defined by its posts and framework, Wade purposely hung no artwork over the head of the bed.

WHAT THE PROS KNOW ABOUT
BRINGING FLOWERS INDOORS

Their rooms may be governed by symmetry, but Patrick Wade and David DeMattei like their flowers on the exuberant side: bursting from the vase, or cascading over the rim. Yet this fresh-from-the-garden look eludes many people, says Patty Wilkerson, owner of San Francisco's Fleur de Mer, who supplies Wade and DeMattei's flowers. "Rigid arrangements are a result of anxiety," she explains. "People have a real fear of cutting stems short. But flowers are more forgiving than you think." She starts a bouquet with a few tall stems, then adds progressively shorter stems until blossoms touch or spill over the edge of the vase, all the way around. Often, she ends up trimming down the tallest flowers, aiming for fullness, not height. Among her trade secrets:

- For a foolproof arrangement, mix hydrangeas, roses, and Queen Anne's lace; it looks beautiful and extravagant.

- Make a tabletop garden with a flat of wheatgrass, a fistful of poppies, and florist's tubes. Fill tubes with water and "plant" in the wheat-grass soil. Insert poppies.

- Wrap long strands of smilax, a delicate vine, around votive candles, wineglasses, even the chandelier. Grow it with caution (it's invasive) or order from a florist.

- Prowl the garden for branches and greens. Remember, some of the loveliest bouquets have no flowers at all.

Top right: For continuity, even a powder room gets the same ivory linen window shade as the public rooms.
Right: In the master bath, twin medicine cabinets were made to look like formally framed mirrors, and positioned to capture natural light.

NORTHWEST

CRAFTED FROM LOCAL MATERIALS OR
BEJEWELED WITH ANTIQUE TILES,
THESE HOUSES, TRANSFORMED, RESPOND
TO GRAY SKIES WITH AN INNER GLOW

53

AN ARCHITECTURAL HOMAGE TO NATURE

The top of this hill on San Juan Island, off the coast of Washington, offers boundless water views—and an obvious site for a house. But Tom Bosworth, a Seattle architect, and his wife, Elaine, an interior designer and antiques dealer, decided to build their weekend home lower down, on a natural ledge in the slope. "It's a happy fit," says Tom, "as if the landscape had been prepared to receive a building here. The house looks like it's growing out of the land."

His design decisions all seem calculated to honor nature, not architecture. To give the house a stony color like the rocky patches around it, Bosworth used unpigmented concrete and cedar that weathers to gray. He dead-ended the driveway some distance away, forcing visitors to abandon their automobiles (and their city tensions) under a stand of trees. As the footpath approaches the house, cars recede from view; solitude and wilderness take over to the point that not a single window requires curtains. The front portico, as if to underscore the architect's sense of reverence, looks like a diminutive temple.

Inside, a Shaker simplicity restrains the rooms. The moldings are broad bands of wood, unadorned. Windows, a monumental $7\frac{1}{2}$ feet tall, have unpainted frames. As for the hearth, a statuesque $6\frac{1}{2}$ feet high, it is cast in stark concrete. In lieu of curves or carvings, it has only

Right: When stone proved too expensive for the portico's steps, Tom Bosworth used concrete and wood. A footpath from the parking area and gatehouse ends at the far side of the portico. The four cedar steps in front lead nowhere, as the hill slopes abruptly and impassably downward.

Above: Elaine Bosworth mixed a folding table purchased in Paris with a Pier 1 wicker chair in the living room. The floorboards are antique 10-inch-wide planks that were cleaned (but not sanded), sealed once, lightly rubbed with stain, then sealed twice more—a light-handed treatment that kept them rustic-looking, but still protected.
Right: To funnel sunlight into a hall, Bosworth raised a windowed monitor above the roofline like a miniature second story. **Opposite:** The master bedroom's plank-style moldings are precisely aligned with the window frames. In a characteristic mix of new and antique, Elaine hung a contemporary quilt at the head of the bed and set an old sea captain's chest at the foot.

a flat frieze that reiterates the molding—yet the nobility of its dimensions invites the gaze to linger. "Proportions are everything," says Tom, "in a building this reserved."

And also this small. The Bosworths divided their 1,070 square feet into two major rooms: one for eating, dining, and relaxing—which consumes the front half of the house—and the second, in back, for sleeping. In every corner, a craving for light is satisfied. Tom banished overhead kitchen cupboards, making space for a bank of windows, then ran open shelves across the glass. A few feet away, he illuminated a potentially dark hallway by raising its ceiling to 22 feet and capping it with a monitor, a windowed structure that thrusts through the roof like a small, empty tower. "Depending on the hour, the sun streaks in at an angle from one direction or the other," he says. "So the time of day is always marked upon the walls."

WHAT THE PROS KNOW ABOUT
OPEN SHELVING

Exposed kitchen shelving is not just about storage—it's about display, and therefore works best when certain rules of order are followed. First, line up the shelves with the window mullions to avoid visual clutter. Second, establish a rigorous palette. Interior designer Elaine Bosworth keeps only her whiteware on view (with a few yellow bowls in one corner for a single shot of color). Third, let the objects breathe. The arrangement is right when it looks relaxed, not rigid; this is, after all, a working kitchen. These exposed shelves are built into the structure of the house. To construct each inch-thick shelf, Tom Bosworth devised a sandwich of two boards supported by a series of L-shaped steel brackets. He hid one end of each L between the boards, bolted the other end to the wall studs nearest the windows, then nailed up the window molding to conceal the brackets. Finally, he edged the front of each shelf with a strip of lath. For a durable, easy-to-clean finish, apply an oil-based primer, then a mildew-inhibiting acrylic paint such as Janovic's ArmorWall Kitchen & Bath Enamel or Zinsser's Perma-White Bathroom Wall & Ceiling Paint.

Left: Designed by Tom, the dining table in the kitchen area has Shaker-like tapering legs and a nine-foot top of salvaged teak from Java. Elaine found the turn-of-the-century tavern chairs for $2.50 apiece. Below-counter cabinet doors are painted white, like the walls, to keep attention focused on tall windows that seem to "disappear" below the back of the countertop.

RESTORING A SPLIT-LEVEL TO ITS PRAIRIE PAST

Seattle architect Tom McCallum calls it the "builder-burger"—the typical 1950s split-level house that looks factory-made no matter where it stands. Its problem, he says, is that postwar developers abandoned the burger's aesthetic roots: the Arts and Crafts bungalow, with its horizontal lines and deep eaves, and the Prairie house, distinguished by low, sloping rooflines and rhythmic bands of trim.

It took only a cursory look at the floor plan for McCallum to show John Zevenbergen, a builder, and his wife, Nancy, a financial adviser, how their suburban Seattle split-level could adopt a sense of the past. First, the architect erased an exterior wall of glass that had made a fishbowl of the living room. He rubbed out several interior walls and relocated a sandstone fireplace that loomed in the middle of the house, interrupting the flow of space. Finally, he penciled in a sense of spatial magnanimity by organizing the first-floor living area into two great rooms, one for cooking and eating, the other for gathering. "That was Thursday," the architect recalls. "By Monday, John had completely gutted the place."

As fast as McCallum could pencil in the details and fax him drawings, Zevenbergen rebuilt, bringing balance and warmth to rooms that had long felt off-center and cold. He took down the glass wall and installed Mission-style custom windows throughout the house. He carved the shed ceilings (which sloped up, but not back down) into more classical shapes, giving one a cathedral-like peak, the other an arch. He built the new hearth that McCallum designed for the living room, its sides striped with long, curving bands of cherry shaped like archers' bows.

Above: The living-room fireplace, designed by architect Tom McCallum, is faced with new tile made in the Arts and Crafts style. The arch in the ceiling is paneled with fir and illuminated with concealed strip lighting, drawing the eye up. **Left:** Patterns on the exterior of the renovated house—in the window mullions, the river stones, and the alternating wide and skinny bands of shingles—establish an intimate scale that suggests an older structure. Windows are framed with double rows of wood strips, the kind of subdued, linear detailing known as carpenter art.

Those rounded lines of woodwork negated the angular character of the house, as did the arch of the ceiling directly overhead. They also liberated the mission-style windows from any association with the small, cloistered bungalow rooms of that period and allowed the space to breathe. "Once I popped that little curveball into the dead space of the ceiling," says McCallum, "you couldn't tell it was a split-level at all."

Materials were chosen for simplicity and inner glow: cherry and Douglas fir, which practically kindle their own amber light, and stainless steel, which speaks honestly of the kitchen's purpose. River stones, which tumble down from the Cascade Range, now sheathe the new chimney and bejewel the base of the entire house. These smooth stones can still be seen on Seattle's Arts and Crafts–era houses—as can some of the smallest artisan-made touches that McCallum borrowed, like the groove routed along the edge of the kitchen's oval island. "The American craftsman was trying to do a simple man's palace with relatively inexpensive materials," McCallum says.

His own goal, more than a century later, was not so different. "We took a manufactured house," he says, "and turned it into a handmade object."

Top left: Because only an island stands between the open kitchen and the dining room, McCallum hinted at the division of space by changing the ceiling styles: flat over the kitchen, pitched over the dining area. The merger of numerous small rooms allowed for a reading corner, with sofa, just off the kitchen. **Far left:** Glass inserts in the kitchen cabinets come to the same rooflike peak as the cathedral ceiling over the dining table. **Left:** The dining area, mapped out by a border of cherry inlay in the new oak floors, faces a door to the garden; the floor-to-ceiling china cabinet, at right, walls off a foyer. The wide aperture between the dining area and the living room just beyond keeps family members within view of each other.

WHAT THE PROS KNOW ABOUT
OPEN KITCHENS

A kitchen that merges with a dining room will also share its needs—for warmth, comfort, a sense of polish. "It can't look clinically hygienic," says architect Tom McCallum, who furnished this Seattle kitchen's sunniest corner with a banquette and coffee table. McCallum won't rule out cold materials like stainless steel, used here on countertops, but he balances them with high-touch elements, like reproduction Arts and Crafts tile. "Stainless can look soft when it's stitched in with other colors," says McCallum. Cabinetry merits the same detailing here as it would in the living room: note the groove routed around the edge of the island's butcher-block top (a Craftsman touch borrowed from old local houses) and the soffit made not of wallboard, but of glowing cherry wood.

A LITTLE HOUSE AMPLIFIED BY PULSING COLOR

Northwesterners fight their overcast skies with pale colors, so their rooms tend to reflect light rather than soak it up. "Our beiges and greiges are so sophisticated," says Joe McDonnal, owner of The Ruins, a Seattle dining club and caterer. "So calming. But when it's time to pick out paint, I go for reds and oranges and yellows, all at the same time."

He lives in a 1904 gabled farmhouse that struck him with its "romantic integrity," particularly in a neighborhood of 1940s and 1950s bungalows. Inside, however, it offered a quarrelsome layout—700 square feet apportioned into seven rooms—until McDonnal went at it with a sledgehammer, and architect Tom McCallum added 500 square feet for an expanded kitchen. "I created the edges of an envelope, and put columns and holes in it," McCallum says. "But all the colors and finishes were Joe's, and he's marvelously irreverent."

McDonnal painted his wood floors in various shades of faded yellow, and striped his living-room walls in marigold, caramel, and terra-cotta—colors that may not reflect daylight, but do generate their own glow in its presence. He drew this Mediterranean palette from a cache of 225 red, saffron, and black tiles salvaged from an abandoned, half-collapsed villa just north of Florence. McDonnal had spent three days prying the tiles up, eight months waiting for the shipment to arrive home, and eight years wondering how to use the treasure stored in his basement. "When we renovated, the tiles were our jumping-off point," he says. McCallum drew the tile designs on paper, made scaled-down photocopies, kaleidoscoped them into patterns—and transformed the floor of an 80-year-old Italian villa into a dining-room wall in Seattle.

Left: Indonesian wooden screens, painted white and widened slightly with bits of wood, let sunlight penetrate the living-room windows while thwarting glances from the street. To create the fishtail curtains, McDonnal made two ungathered, bannerlike panels for each window, then pinned the inside bottom corner of each panel up and back toward the opposite corner. The tassels are from Laos. **Above:** To animate traditional furnishings, McDonnal adds quirks—like a wing chair dressed differently from its mate, or a coffee table with curvy, cast-iron legs.

WHAT THE PROS KNOW ABOUT
HAND-STRIPED WALLS

The stripes on Joe McDonnal's living-room walls are layered with glazes in two to five hues. Seattle interior designer David Staskowski achieves similar drama with flat latex paint and his own forgiving recipe.

- Over primed walls, apply two coats of marigold paint (Benjamin Moore no. 145).

- Map out five-inch-wide stripes, five inches apart: lean a tall, one-by-three piece of wood against the wall; check straightness with a level, and make pencil dots (not lines) on the wall to denote edges of stripes.

- Paint every other stripe with a wash of half water, half caramel-colored paint (no. 126) and a wide, flat synthetic brush. Work from the ceiling down, then stroke, with a nearly dry brush, from the bottom up.

- When dry, paint ribbon-thin stripes with a wash of half water, half terra-cotta paint (no. 077) and a round, pointed-tip brush. Run the ribbons along the seams between the marigold and caramel stripes.

- Top-wash the wall with Benjamin Moore Latex Glazing Liquid, lightly tinted (1 tablespoon terra-cotta paint to 1 cup glaze). *Tip:* Washes are runny; protect baseboards with blue painter's tape.

Opposite: The dining room mantel is a ledge of rock supported by a pair of French Provincial gargoyles. To give this long, narrow room more architectural complexity, McDonnal pinstriped the ceiling beams with dark red and black glazes. **Above:** The bumped-out kitchen had no room for a back staircase until architect Tom McCallum threaded in a prefabricated, 60-inch-wide spiral stair. The wicker table looked awkward against the built-in cabinetry until McDonnal painted it the same butter yellow as the ceiling and walls. **Above right:** To spare a prize pear tree, the breakfast room could be no larger than eight feet by seven feet. To satisfy McDonnal's lifelong desire to have a house with a turret, McCallum made it octagonal, with six light-filled windows. Painting the English Victorian table white gave it the simplicity of old lace.

MIDWEST

DETAILED WITH SALVAGED WOOD
OR ANCIENT BOISERIE, BUILT NEW OR
BARELY WIRED FOR ELECTRICITY,
THESE HOMES EMBRACE AN OLD-WORLD
RESTRAINT AND PRIDE OF PLACE

69

Forty acres of good land. That was the selling point—certainly not the abandoned brick house bereft of wiring and running water. Yet in this uninsulated relic in Montrose, Minnesota, about 40 miles west of Minneapolis, James Hanson perceived good bones and gently formal rooms. "It was scarred up, but unaltered," he recalls. And like many farmhouses, it told an old story of a growing family: the center section built in 1867, the left wing constructed a generation later, in 1896.

Hanson moved in amid the rubble, a gentleman farmer with power tools and a respect for history. He and Stephen Douthit—designers, artisans, and co-owners of the Minneapolis store American Island, where they sell antique and weathered furniture—not only restored the house, but balanced it out with a second wing. The new 20-by-30-foot conservatory lacks a glass roof, in deference to the northern climate, but it has the spirit of a greenhouse. Indeed, the partners bought the glass before they framed out the room: $8,000 worth of doors and transoms (actually panels for patio doors) for a bargain $1,500, thanks to a surplus-window supplier. The height of the ceiling, determined by the top of the transoms, came to 12 feet.

The house is furnished with an eye to elegance—and flaws. The conservatory's poured concrete

Left: The farmhouse, with new wing at right. The original structure was altered only where a living-room window was replaced with a new front door. **Right:** In the conservatory addition, Hanson made the room's vivid woodwork from the cheapest pine he could find.

floor, for example, was painted in a diamond pattern with ordinary latex paint, and mildly protected with matte polyurethane. "We *wanted* it to get scuffed," explains Douthit. "That's our whole philosophy. We like to see the mistakes and the age and the quirks in things." Some of their best pieces have an eccentric provenance, like the "blood auction," a house sale where the furniture bore stickers from the sheriff's office and generous splashes of blood. Unblinking, Hanson and Douthit bought a voluptuous tufted Victorian sofa for $10, rebuilt it, and re-covered it in jade velvet. Explains Douthit: "We love the huge bun feet."

In their only major change to the original structure, they now use the old living room as a generous front hall. It is lit by a 1930s iron chandelier that turned up, rusted but electrified, at a Chicago flea market. Douthit "restored" it with the same kind of reverence he and Hanson brought to the house itself: by snaking out the wires, installing candles, and leaving the rust untouched.

Far left: Turn-of-the-century American glass beadwork, originally made to frame a doorway, hangs in the conservatory entrance. The shapely wicker table was a castoff from Douthit's parents; the kilim, at right, from Hanson's. Douthit made the Wardian case, a diminutive greenhouse in the late-Victorian style, at left. **Left:** The partners dressed up an old voting table with a weathered green finish and gilt highlights. The top (with a brass slot for ballots) was damaged, so they made a new one: inlaid squares of plywood, painted white—with the excess rubbed off for instant aging.

WHAT THE PROS KNOW ABOUT
COLLECTING EARLY
PHOTOGRAPHS

A big-eared man holding a seedling, a woman with her prize cow: Jim Hanson and Steve Douthit are passionate collectors of old snapshot portraits showing "people with pride in their faces." Collecting by category, as they do, can be amazingly inexpensive. Snapshots and studio portraits from the early 20th century cost as little as $1 at flea markets (though older forms, like daguerreotypes, are rarer and pricier). "Photos of black and Native American subjects and immigrants—people who document our history—are rising in value," says author Pat Ross, whose own collection appears in her book *The Kinship of Women*. So are pictures of Victorian home interiors, natural disasters, and pets. Collect for love, not resale, Ross advises: look for evocative images with a pleasing sense of composition.

Left: The 12 or 13 layers of wallpaper on one foyer wall nearly defeated Hanson. With a circular saw, he scored the paper with the outlines of a stone wall, then rubbed on a rocky finish with paint. **Above:** Early photographs, including a photo of the farmhouse, circa 1910, hang above the mantel.

Opposite: The hearth in the dining room, made of salvaged wood, was added to give the room a focal point; its fake firebox is concealed with a piece of antique crewelwork. The seascape was a flea-market find.
Left: In one of the conservatory's three gathering spots, a 1928 painting of Pocahontas hangs near a Victorian-era stuffed Chihuahua in a glass case. But modern-day objects, if sufficiently curious, are acceptable, too—like the elephant-head brackets, purchased in a furniture store. **Above:** In the workshop, nails and other objects are stashed in a chest made by a caretaker in the 1920s.

WHAT THE PROS KNOW ABOUT
COLLECTING OLD SILVER

Hanson and Douthit rarely polish their vintage silver, and don't even own a price guide. "We collect whimsical shapes," says Douthit, "and pieces with personal meaning." The silver-plated ballet slippers were a gift to Hanson, who studied dance; other objects, like sterling cups from 1930s animal shows, are pleasingly quirky (and make good vases). To find the affordable and the unusual in sterling, Houston dealer Phyllis Tucker suggests small, vintage pieces that were intimately used, from compacts to flatware to Japanese cigarette boxes. American silverplate, long ignored by "serious" collectors, offers marvelous eccentricities. Collectors of silver plate have also started buying vintage hotel silver—a silver-over-nickel mix used for serving pieces because it tarnished slowly and wore well. Tucker's tip: if an item needs replating, either pass it up or live with the worn spots; poorly done, the replating can ruin the piece.

Far left: The kitchen's dining corner is furnished with simple, slightly crude pieces: a vintage cabinet, painted by the homeowners; a set of primitive Windsor chairs, painted generations ago in different colors; and a late-19th-century table from a client's basement. **Above left:** Old silver, displayed in the dining room, is collected for its fanciful looks. Hanson and Douthit built the shelving of salvaged wood, then gave it "one intentionally bad coat of paint." **Left:** Kitchen cupboards were made with barn windows, purchased at a local lumberyard; they offered divided panes of glass at a low cost. Brown and white ironstone dishes, mostly mismatched, are displayed inside. "Surge" is an old brand of milking machine.

NATURAL FINDS AND FORMAL BONES

Peg Fetter and Stuart Kendall live in a five-room, turn-of-the-century shotgun apartment above a soul food restaurant in south St. Louis. It has landlord-white walls, which as renters they have learned to ignore. But it also stands on ceremony, with pocket doors between the rooms, and pilasters at the hearth. "It's conducive to formality," says Fetter.

Why, then, is the prestigious spot over the mantel held by a gnarled, knotted tangle of roots?

"Stuart pulled it out of a river," confesses Fetter, "and we thought it looked just fabulous, like a weaving." An artist and designer, she, too, shops the wilderness when she isn't scouring antique shops. Here, chandeliers get strung with thorns, the frames of paintings crowned with autumn leaves—and the apartment, with its unruly touches of nature, has lost the starch of its Victorian past and the neutrality of its vanilla walls.

Fetter has a master's degree in metalsmithing, and designs everything from jewelry to the steel ottoman with a bulldog stance that gleams in her living room. Through their home-design shop, Celadon, Fetter and Kendall sell Asian furnishings, Fortuny lanterns, Fetter's paintings and furniture, and artisan-made objects and jewelry—"fabulous things that I can't easily find in St. Louis," Fetter says.

What she does find, she alters with artistic license: the Chinese art deco rug, tossed down at a slant as if to defy her solemn hearth, or the dining room's Chippendale-style chairs, whose white seats she silk-screened with black bats. "I've never followed a decorating theme in my life," Fetter says. "If we like something enough, it works."

Above: The living room is a highly personal gallery of local talent: a steel console table, dripping with tiny crosses, by David Weitz; the painting above it, by Alaina Genakos; and, on the small easel at left, a painting of plums, by Peg Fetter. The white chairs are secondhand finds, re-covered. **Far left:** Two paintings by Brad Aldridge, purchased in Hot Springs, Arizona, hang in the dining room. **Left:** A length of wool from Kashmir, India, makes an unorthodox tablecloth; a Jamaican mask stirs up the cultural mix.

EMBRACING VENICE IN THE HEART OF CHICAGO

For a long time, interior designer Barbara Lione defined perfection as a Barcelona chair. Growing up in Germany, she loved the rigor of Bauhaus design; transplanted to Chicago, she revered the modern skyline. But over years of travel, Venice seeped into her blood, and one day she realized she was in love—with gilded mirrors, Fortuny fabric, endlessly tall French doors.

The Chicago town house that Lione and her husband, Richard, commissioned from architect Larry Booth is a mirror of both allegiances. A pared-down urban villa, it is laid out on the European plan: large entrance hall on the ground floor, a piano with the public rooms one flight up, and bedrooms at the top. (As a reward for climbing stairs, guests get a view of trees, not traffic.) Because Lione envisioned her 18th-century antiques against the foil of a gallery-like setting, Booth gave her walls without moldings, windows without mullions, rooms unconfined by doors. Proportion, not detail, creates the elegance here: twin salons on the second floor—one a living room, the other a kitchen and sitting room combined—are 32 feet long, with ceilings a magnanimous 12 feet high. "I want people circulating around me when I cook," Lione told her architect, and as a result, one space flows easily into the next through expansive five-foot apertures.

Right: The rear addition by architect Richard Gibbons has a facade that matches the front of the house, designed by architect Larry Booth. Landscape architect Craig Bergmann surrounded a bluestone dining terrace, at right, with beds of lavender, ivy, and thyme. The result: an outdoor room that requires no mowing.

She embellished her clean-cut living room with a carved French fireplace, her sitting room with a French wedding armoire. In both salons, she glazed the walls a strawlike yellow she had often seen in Italy. Yet over the years, with her Barcelona chairs long supplanted by French and Italian antiques, Lione found herself yearning for old-world room surroundings—a corner of the house where she could present a formal dinner, a library warmed with the presence of books and made intimate by a door she could close.

Ten years after the town house was built, formality—in the form of doors, moldings, and limestone-and-marble floors—arrived with a two-story rear addition that faces her city garden. Designed by architect Richard Gibbons, it holds a library on the ground floor and an octagonal dining room above. Lione bought a cache of 18th-century French boiserie, or wall paneling, at auction for the library, and retreats to the new rooms when she craves a sense of ceremony.

For all its romance, the town house remains restful on the eyes. Sofas and chairs are neatly dressed in white. Paintings hang alone, never jostling for space on the walls. And Lione honors every object with plenty of breathing room—a lingering trace, perhaps, of her modernist roots.

Left: The Bessarabian rug in Lione's living room, the flourish of a mirror over her hearth, and walls that are glazed instead of painted, all combine to give the room an instant history. Lione chose a glass-topped coffee table that would neither masquerade as something old nor look ponderous amid the antiques. **Right:** English-style chairs in the sitting room, like many upholstered pieces in the house, are covered in chenille. Lione prefers custom-made seating over antique for its higher comfort level. The 1812 French armoire anchors a symmetrical arrangement of furniture and art.

WHAT THE PROS KNOW ABOUT
LIGHTING A LIBRARY

Remember reading in bed with a flashlight? An adult with a book not only needs more light, but needs it from two sources simultaneously, says Sara Schrager, a partner in Warfel Schrager Architectural Lighting of Connecticut. *Ambient lighting,* which softly illuminates the whole room, prevents the flashlight-under-the-covers glare of a bright lamp in dim surroundings. Because library walls are traditionally paneled or dark, bounce light off a white ceiling with a halogen torchère or sconce. *Task lighting,* which shines directly on the page, can come from table lamps, desktop halogen lamps, or that hinged classic, the architect's lamp. Position the task light so it comes from above and over your left shoulder (if you are right-handed; reverse if left-handed), and have the lower edge of the shade at eye level to avoid glare.

Top: The new dining room, an octagon, makes a beveled showcase for four prized panels of antique Italian wallpaper. Lione had cabinets built beneath each panel and stippled the wood green. Beyond the Regency table and chairs, a small dining terrace is visible. **Above:** Opera-style draperies in the dining room are pulled back by a cord hidden in the lining. **Right:** New doors in the library were faux-painted—down to their trompe l'oeil decorative moldings—to match the 18th-century oak boiserie on the library walls. **Far right:** The library's wicker sofa and chairs, deep and overscaled, invite relaxation in an otherwise dressy room.

LIVING IN
A STATE OF GRACE

Bruce Schabell and Tim Foster are the gentle stewards of a four-room, pre–Civil War house built by Swedish settlers in Stockholm, Wisconsin. Most of its walls have never seen paint— only a single layer of wallpaper, applied decades ago. The house had been vacant more than 50 years when Schabell and Foster bought it, and the wallpaper had fallen away in dusty sheets, revealing mottled, virgin plaster. Occasionally, a visitor asks when they plan to paint. But the owners have no intention of disturbing this restful vignette of the past: "The walls have a beauty of their own," says Schabell, a decorative artist. "They haven't been painted in the history of the house, so I feel that they shouldn't be. Not by me, anyway."

Indeed, the owners' intervention has been so delicate that the house, used mostly on summer weekends, still has no indoor plumbing. (Showers are taken at a nearby hotel, owned by Foster's aunt; water comes from bottles, or a nearby well.) For a while there was no electricity, either, until the cost of candles became impractical; even now, wiring is minimal, and involves extension cords. Heat is supplied by two cast-iron stoves, and without a phone in the house, conversations ramble on, uninterrupted. Rooms are blanketed by serenity—though the hush seems intrinsic to Stockholm, too (population 89).

The stark interior has grown elegant as Schabell and Foster, perceiving a certain nobility in the house, responded to it in their decorating. Their Gustavian-style furnishings have delicately fluted legs. Chippendale ladder-back chairs stand at the kitchen farm table. An unwired crys-

Left: The Louis XVI–style settee in the downstairs dining room was expelled from a fur salon; the flea-market trunks beside it, essential in a house without closets, store firewood and other articles. **Top:** The formal garden in front of the house is planted with yew and boxwood. **Above:** A fat silk tassel from a film set now dangles from a French door in the upstairs parlor.

tal chandelier glitters in the upstairs parlor, and Schabell unrolled a floorcloth in the kitchen that resembles inlaid marble. "I love the mix of something provincial and something palatial," he explains. He and Foster derived even their garden layout from French and Italian villas, planting it with a round fountain, grassy avenues, and flawless symmetry. "The garden seemed to fit the house, which is tall and symmetrical and sits up on a hill," says Schabell. "Height always gives you the best vantage point for viewing a formal garden."

Of the four rooms—bedroom and parlor upstairs, kitchen and dining below—only one called out for cosmetic work. "The dining room had been painted in an awful green enamel, and the wallpaper over that would not strip easily," says Schabell. He hid the offense behind a pale yellow parchment glaze, dabbed on with cheesecloth, then allowed himself a harlequin pattern painted directly on the parlor floor. Since then, he and Foster have refused to treat the house as a canvas, intruding on it only lightly and only for its own good: protective shutters, new windows, paint for the clapboard exterior. Restraint, rather than renovation, has restored their home to a state of grace.

Left: The owners' laissez-faire policy extends to the dining-room linoleum, installed in the 1930s. The table dates to the late 1860s; the vintage lantern above it was payment for one of Schabell's decorative-painting jobs.
Overleaf: Tim Foster resuscitated the parlor's Salvation Army "motel lamp," at right, by binding its tall aluminum base with poplar branches. For a center table, he and Schabell topped a cast-iron urn with a round of fossilized stone. The Baker daybed is probably from the 1960s.

WHAT THE PROS KNOW ABOUT
FLOORCLOTHS

Bruce Schabell lavishes his floorcloths with faux marbling, but these painted canvas carpets also blossom under simple treatments. Paint freehand or choose a forgiving design, so minor flaws won't be a crisis, advises Schabell. He works with acrylic paints, which resist cracking and go on easily with brushes, rags, or faux-finishing tools. Tack the canvas to a floor to make it taut while you paint. Seal with four coats of waterborne polyurethane; reseal as signs of wear appear. Roll, don't fold, to transport. The cloth itself is 11-ounce cotton canvas: prime it twice on each side with acrylic gesso, or order preprimed floorcloths from Pearl Paint in New York City (800.221.6845). For more information: *The Complete Book of Floorcloths*, by Kathy Cooper and Jan Hersey (Lark Books).

Above and right: The kitchen floorcloth is a fantastical mix of painted marble, granite, and slate, a heady contrast to the scarred walls. **Opposite:** A turn-of-the-century winterscape painting, unsigned, hangs at left in the sole bedroom.

TEXAS AND THE SOUTHWEST

THIS IS THE LAND OF THE GRAND
GESTURE: EVEN WHEN PARED TO THE
BONE WITH AN ELEGANT ECONOMY,
THESE HOUSES THINK BIG

97

GIVERNY
IN A DUSTY
LANDSCAPE

The Southwest is built of luscious mud—of adobe bricks in buff and ocher, mocha and rust. Maurice Dixon, a New Mexico painter, tinsmith, and color consultant, loves the stuff; he built much of his house by himself, laying 15,000 bricks by hand. (Friends were invited to a mud-slinging party to help.)

But in this dusty landscape, where natural adobe gets its blush from iron oxide, Dixon's home stands out for its hothouse colors. Its garden is planted in the passionate style of Giverny, with a blaze of nasturtiums, geraniums, lavender, and hollyhocks. And its rooms are saturated in the violets and greens of antique Mexican glazes, inspired by Dixon's pottery collection. Around Santa Fe, where adobe houses come in desert tones, this is startling splendor.

Before Dixon's laying-on of hands, the 1870 house was a two-room Territorial structure—an established hybrid of rudimentary adobe style, which accounts for its thick walls, low horizons, and Greek Revival detailing (an American passion at the time). Dixon added a *sala,* or great room; a library; a bedroom; an entry atrium with a glass ceiling; a private chapel, or *oratorio;* and two *portals*, or covered porches—all in similar Territorial style. Foundations were dug with a shovel. ("I don't like machines," the artist says.) He let the rooms ramble, one into the next, as if each had been added on a need-to-grow basis; those not "winterized" with fireplaces are reserved for warm-weather use.

The rooms were also planned around his collection of antique and salvaged doors, many of them from Mexico. As a result, most doorways in this house are treated like frames, both for

Left: The original 19th-century *portal* is more of a passageway than a porch, and serves as a greenhouse for shade-loving plants. One of six entrances to the house, it flanks the kitchen, dining room, and central hall. **Top:** The open-air *portal* out back is similar to one Dixon saw in a Oaxaca hotel. The blue and yellow Mexican door, circa 1850, leads to a private chapel. Exterior plaster walls are sponged with rose-colored paint that was watered down for a faded appearance. **Above:** The original section of the house, dating to 1870, is fitted with a Victorian-era Mexican screened door. Century-old brick coping on the roof mimics classical dentil molding.

an enticing slice of the room beyond and for the door itself. "Doors are sculpture," says Dixon. "They have architecture, craftsmanship, and color, especially when they've weathered." In many cases, he crowns them—with an old beam for a lintel, or a painted design, or the primitive power of a handmade mesquite cross.

The kitchen is a working museum, with Mexican and Spanish ceramics not only displayed but used every day. The ancient-looking *saltillo* tile floor is in fact new but was not allowed to remain in that state for long: Dixon sponged it with water-soluble red and brown paint and pigments, which the *saltillo,* being bisque, like a flowerpot, absorbed. "When it had a dirty look to it, I sealed it with burnt-umber-tinted varnish," he says. "The rest of the aging process was just use."

Because the artist paints his walls much as he arranges flowers—depending on the mood and the moment—dazzling greens, purples, and blues come and go quickly in these rooms. Dixon used ultra-deep hues by Wellborn, an Albuquerque company that supersaturates some of its colors with pigments until they seem to generate their own pulse. "If I acquire something new, that's reason to repaint," says Dixon. "The more color, the better. Houses should be joyous."

Opposite: Dixon paneled the kitchen workstation with unadorned tin, a declaration of love from the artist to his raw material. The kitchen, which has stood in this spot since the house was built, is equipped with little more than a stove, sink, and refrigerator, and a pot rack of the owner's design. **Left:** Late-19th-century sieves from Spain or Portugal, made with stretched and punched goatskin, hang in the entry atrium. Dixon cut and decorated 200 pieces of metal to make the two scrolled candelabra on the antique Mexican table.

WHAT THE PROS KNOW ABOUT
TESTING COLOR BEFORE YOU PAINT

Every shade of paint has multiple personalities, depending on whether you view it as a chip, in the can, or on a sunny wall. To avoid surprises, test color where you plan to apply it. Off-white walls will throw off your perception—so paint the room with primer first for a nearly pure white backdrop, *then* test, advises Neil Janovic of Janovic/Plaza Decorating Centers. (The primer also yields a more polished paint job in the end.) A good-sized test swatch is four feet square, with ample white space between different colors. New York architect Michael McDonough brushes test swatches on a room's darkest wall (typically the one with windows), the brightest wall (where sunlight lands), near floor-level close to carpets and wood (to see how the hues interact), and in every type of light used in the room —incandescent, fluorescent, or halogen. (In certain light, even deep burgundy can look fire-engine red.) Other pros make movable swatches, using cardboard sold for this purpose by paint stores, or simply the backs of Wet Paint signs. A key advantage: paper swatches can be taken with you on fabric-shopping expeditions.

Above right: In the sunroom, just off the kitchen, plates from 1920s Oaxaca are distinguished by splashy cobalt dahlias. The table, a slatted *equipal* from Mexico, has a pig-hide top; it is Dixon's favorite spot for working and eating. **Right:** A view of the recently added *sala,* or great room, from a "transition room" in the original house. **Opposite:** Over the *sala*'s 19th-century doors, salvaged from a hacienda, Dixon painted a cloudburst; the design adds ceremony, height, and a touch of the artist's hand. Like antique doors in other rooms, these are burnished with paste wax to give them luster without shine.

PEELING AND TARNISHED ... BUT GRANDEUR ALL THE SAME

On the south side of San Antonio, on the top floor of a three-story 1880s warehouse that once stored seeds, Gwynn Griffith lives in what can only be described as a half-ruined European villa. Her foyer chandelier may be French crystal, but chunks of plaster have fallen from the living-room walls. She reads to the light of a glittering Baccarat lamp, but her century-old floor-boards go resolutely unpolished. And while she loves her antique Oushak rug, it's in the kitchen—where she turns it periodically so stains are distributed evenly.

"I don't treat things like they're precious," says Griffith, an interior designer known for her love of old textiles, statuesque architecture, and grand, but slightly worn, antiques. "And I don't care if a thing goes with everything else, as long as I like it."

When Griffith moved in, she stashed a burgeoning collection of antiques on the lower two floors, then confronted the 4,000 square feet where she planned to live and work: a stadium-sized box with 13-foot ceilings and 31 windows, but inadequate wiring and no interior walls.

Left: The seed warehouse is now Gwynn Griffith's home, office, and storage site for antiques. **Right:** In the foyer, around the corner from the freight elevator, an 18th-century faux-grained chest from France stands on 1880s floorboards that Griffith had carefully cleaned, but not varnished or waxed. The red columns are from a salvage shop, as are the doors; Griffith found them stripped of their paint and left them as is.

Among her furnishings were salvaged columns and 10-foot-high French doors, elements to be embraced by the new construction. "I figured out where to put walls as I went," the designer says. I used to think if a wall was there, that's where it stayed. But with a big space like this, putting up walls turned out to be one of the cheapest things I could do."

Griffith engaged one of her sons, muralist Greg Mannino, to glaze the new walls in a manner inspired more by old Italian villas than by the Spanish missions of Texas. The four exterior walls, all original to the building, she distressed herself by chipping plaster off the brick near the windows. It looked romantic, but it also taught her a lesson: "The plaster was there for a reason," she says, pointing to the chinks and cracks that have developed. "That brick is so old it wasn't fired, so when the wind blows, the brick deteriorates into dust."

Her living room, lit by countless pools of lamplight, is a convention of antique chairs, some covered in new Fortuny fabric and the rest in old textiles, often cut from antique drapery. In a grand gesture, she once upholstered a Charles X chair with the healthy sections of a damaged Aubusson rug. "It could have been restored," she sighs, momentarily missing the rug. "I could kick myself." Then her natural irreverence returns, and she points out an 18th-century cherub from Italy, its gilded arms raised to support, at the moment, a television set. "Did you notice its face?" she asks. "Up close, it looks exactly like Richard Nixon."

Left: Griffith left the living room's numerous windows uncurtained to avoid what threatened to be "a solid wall of fabric." An 18th-century Italian writing desk backs up to a Louis XVI sofa, though the walls around them appear to be in decay. **Right:** In a luxuriously overstuffed corner of the living room, Griffith joyously mixes patterns: Fortuny fabric on the late-18th-century French chair, a leopard print on the piano bench, and stripes on the Italian majolica lamp. The painting is by her son, Greg Mannino.

WHAT THE PROS KNOW ABOUT "RUINED" WALLS

Greg Mannino is an artist, not a decorative painter, so he approached his mother's new Sheetrock walls as if they were blank canvases, building up layers of distressed, ambery color. His recipe for ruin uses only water-based paints, making it a fairly easy project. To start, apply a base coat of flat white latex paint. Don't sand or patch cracks beforehand: "Unevenness adds character," Mannino says. Next, mix a runny glaze—roughly one pint of ocher-colored latex paint to one gallon of clear acrylic medium. Brush onto small areas, then pat, rub, and wipe the still-wet glaze with sponges and rags, using both hands to avoid uniformity. (Don't dab; it leaves telltale sponge marks.) For subsequent coats, start with the identical mixture but add small amounts of universal acrylic pigment: Venetian red to the second coat, burnt umber to the third, raw umber to the last. With this final and darkest mixture, create shadows in the corners rather than glazing the entire wall. "The only real mistake you can make," says Mannino, "is making the wall look too perfect."

Left: Because kitchens always draw a crowd, Griffith treats them like good sitting rooms. Her own (like her clients') is furnished with lamps, rugs, draperies, antiques, and art. The table is Mexican, the painted cabinet 18th-century Portuguese, and the curtains a Clarence House print that resembles crewelwork. Griffith had the deep double sink made from scrap marble—"It looks like a sarcophagus for twins." Her major concession to contemporary kitchen design is undercounter lighting.

SANTA FE HYBRID: REMEMBERING THE EAST

When the railroad first thundered into Santa Fe, it carried sawn lumber, tin, and design ideas from the East. Flat-topped adobes sprouted gingerbread trim and Victorian airs. It was this eccentric, century-old mix that Gil and Eileen Hitchcock, married stockbrokers with a passion for old houses, decided to re-create when they built their own home.

They spent a year studying old architectural photographs, braking for dilapidated farmhouses to scrutinize details and construction techniques, and, finally, designing their own historically respectful home. Its East Coast personality comes through in the tall, deep-set windows, the modernized neoclassical lines of the hearth, and even the stately, nine-inch profile of the baseboards, which Eileen endlessly redrew on paper. But the house also honors its pueblo past: under a traditional coat of stucco is a double, insulating layer of adobe bricks.

To give the rooms warmth rather than discernible color, Eileen stirred raw umber into white paint for the walls. She painted furnishings in "dirty" hues that reminded her of the landscape, then left the rooms so uncluttered that a visitor once asked when she planned to unpack. "The house looked beautiful empty," says Eileen. "We tried to retain that quality, so you're always aware of the architectural bones."

Right: The back entry hall serves as a mudroom, striped with a band of Shaker pegs; red woodwork gives the space definition. The turn of a corner conceals a door to the garage.

WHAT THE PROS KNOW ABOUT
HISTORIC PAINTS

The new milk paint on the Hitchcocks' dining chairs is almost what their maker might have used: a solution of milk, water, earth pigments, and lime. "It dries dead flat with a rough texture, and looks old right away," says Charles Thibeau, whose Old Fashioned Milk Paint Company sells the real thing—a powder made with real milk that buyers mix with water. (Another manufacturer, Stulb Co., sells a close reproduction that comes premixed.) Milk paint comes in colors from earlier centuries—think of barn red, mustard, buttermilk beige—and devotees like Hitchcock know all the tricks: rub the paint off slightly around furniture edges or knobs, simulating age; apply wax, not sealer, for an authentic-looking luster. (For more information: Old Fashioned Milk Paint Company, 508.448.6336; Stulb Co., 800.498.7687.)

Opposite: Eileen Hitchcock painted the living-room beams a shiny white, hated it, stripped off as much as she could, and sealed the distressed surface with wax. **Top left:** The deep covered porch, or *portal*, makes a summer dining room. **Left:** Black milk-painted English tavern chairs in the dining room gather at a Shaker-style table.

Driving through San Antonio's inner city, architects David Lake and Ted Flato used to stop to admire a structure of surprising elegance: a cement factory built of steel columns, lanky truss-work, and corrugated sheet metal, all about a century old. "It looked graceful, light, and thin," recalls Flato. So when he and Lake learned that it was being sold as scrap, they urged clients Henry and Francine Carraro to snap up the toolshed—at 180 feet long and 20 feet high, a cross between an industrial warehouse and a cathedral.

Then they reinvented it as a house.

A demolition crew hauled the pieces to the Carraros' spread in an Austin hill-country suburb and reassembled them as a Z-shaped compound. At one end stands an open-air metal car-port. In the middle, a corrugated-metal building houses the master bedroom and library. And at the far end sprawls the largest structure, at 60 feet long—a screened-in porch with walls so translucent and roof so high it could almost be mistaken for a bird sanctuary.

Flato and Lake, who often borrow from vernacular architecture, adapted the spirit of the porch

Left: A dog trot, or breezeway, lined with sheets of steel cuts through the master-bedroom wing. **Above right:** A corrugated, galvanized steel roof has extra-deep undulations; their visible shadows subliminally hint at relief on hot days. **Right:** The screened porch, at right, looms over the rest of the compound.

from the hill country's dance halls—the kind whose walls can be raised in good weather, leaving an open pavilion. Here, where rain sometimes spatters the edges of the floor, the Carraros eat, relax, and entertain. Their kitchen and an indoor living room are sheltered in a sleek limestone building that nests in one corner of the porch, like a little house tucked inside a larger one. "We wanted the stone structure to look heavy," says Flato, "so the steel columns and trusses would feel even lighter."

Because the architecture is adapted to the weather's extremes, the porch requires no heat, no air-conditioning, and no damage control after thunderstorms. In winter, the stone building blocks the north wind. For summer cooling, the peaked ceiling funnels hot air toward a cupola, where it escapes through louvered vents. Rainwater vanishes into the Mexican brick floor, because the bricks were set in sand. And because the Carraros spend most of their time on the porch, only a handful of smaller rooms demand the expense of heating and cooling. Says Flato: "It's an environmentally wise house."

Left: Porch screening is plastic, not metal, because long strips of it had to be sewn together. Inside, meals are eaten at a century-old harvest table nearly 20 feet long. A guest room, atop the stone building, has its own interior terrace; the living room, with a hearth, lies to the right of the stairs. **Right:** A patio outside the bedroom wing is furnished simply, with Adirondack chairs. (To hint at a distinction, outdoor Adirondacks are painted green; those indoors are white.)

Left: Visitors assume that the living-room fireplace, about eight feet wide and deep enough for benches, was rescued from the cement factory; in fact, Lake/Flato designed it to resemble a salvaged hearth. Round coffee tables, especially generous ones, are hard to find; this one was a dining table before it was cut down to size.

Above: Prints by Texan artists, including Jerry Bywaters and Alexander Hogue, hang over the living room's 19th-century American sideboard. The iron candlesticks were also crafted regionally.

WHAT THE PROS KNOW ABOUT
FINDING AND USING
INDUSTRIAL MATERIALS

"This house was built like the Brooklyn Bridge, with rivets and trusses," says Lake/Flato project architect Graham Martin. "The framework might cost $500,000 to make now." (Sold as scrap, however, it cost the Carraros less than $25,000.) Without buying the bones of a building, there are many ways to express the industrial esthetic. Diamond plate, the pressed sheet metal used for sidewalk elevator doors, makes an enduring and exotic floor; so does black textured rubber, with its coin-sized extrusions. Quilted sheet metal moves gracefully from diners to domestic kitchens; perforated steel can cloak a cabinet door; galvanized steel can line a shower stall (a Lake/Flato favorite); and janitors' sinks are deep enough to hide a mess of dishes. Work with an experienced architect or contractor who can avoid errors, like placing slippery metal on a bathroom floor, says Syracuse, New York, architect Elizabeth Kamell. "New materials demand experimentation, and they may be expensive in small quantities," she adds. For inspiration, Kamell suggests commercial catalogs: McNichols Master Catalog (perforated metals, gratings, screening), 800.237.3820; Julius Blum & Co. (handrails, brackets, ornamental metal), 800.526.6293; Johnson Marine (turnbuckles, clamps, and other hardware), 800.343.8294; Häfele Kitchen Solutions (storage products), 800.HAFELE-1.

Above: The master bedroom is an airy shrine to Francine Carraro's girlhood brass bed; her parents plucked it from a 10-foot-high curbside heap of beds, all discarded, as the family story goes, by a Creed, Colorado, house of ill repute. Francine's christening dress hangs on the wall.

Above: Voluptuous turned bedposts on 1940s mahogany twin beds, stationed in the guest room, contrast with the linear framework of the screened porch. The guest room opens onto its own terrace within the larger porch.
Left: The kitchen is anchored by a 1950s Chambers stove that the Carraros found in an antique store. To make space for art, cookbooks, and views, overhead cabinets were omitted; for visual simplicity, drawer pulls were banished.

THE STARTLING
SPRAWL OF AN
INTIMATE HOME

Maybe living in Texas gave Sheridan Lorenz, a lighting designer, and her husband, Perry, a real-estate investor, license to think big. In any event, they did not ask their architects for a house, but for a small village—a rambling structure that would unfold like a tiny walled town, inviting exploration. "Have you ever seen the Peloponnesus?" says Sheridan, who has family in Greece. "Do you know how the roofs of the houses merge if you squint your eyes? I wanted a house that would hug the hillside in that way."

Paul Lamb, the lead architect, and Gary Furman, project architect, laid out a 3,000-square-foot community of limestone rooms and towers and timber annexes, all tucked into this dry central Texas slope. The house is clearly part Texan: its stone was quarried just north of town, its plantings are indigenous, and the structures cascade downhill as if they had clung to this land for centuries. But visitors still seem to be broaching a medieval village, following the walls, terraces, meandering stairs, and mossy paths that ascend to various points of entry.

"It was almost as if they threaded the house through the trees," says Sheridan. "Sometimes I'll wonder, 'Why didn't we make it wider here?' Then I'll look out the window and see a tree, and remember."

Inside, the long front hall feels like an ancient street. It has a stony floor—actually poured concrete, pocked with rock salt—and scabrous limestone walls, as if it might be lined with houses rather than rooms; high in its walls are little windows, mysterious as keyholes, suggesting a secret courtyard on the far side. (In fact, it's the kitchen.) This "street" jogs on in tantalizing

Left: Steps at the rear of the house cascade from a dining bay and nearby kitchen to the garden below. The dry-stack stairs are cut into the hill and laid with stone but no mortar, allowing greenery to sprout in the cracks. **Top:** To pump up an unassuming front entry, the architects designed an archway significantly wider than the path. "It creates a bigger scale," says Lamb. A high, tiny window at left illuminates a powder room. **Above:** A limestone tower to the right of the rear steps holds the living room upstairs and master bedroom below.

fashion: it climbs three steps here, widens there, abruptly narrows, and finally bursts into a miniature plaza—a five-sided chamber of no apparent purpose, except as a place to get one's bearings before entering the living room or kitchen. "From this spot," says Sheridan, "you can see every material we put into the house—the forged sconces, the concrete floors, and both the rough and polished limestone."

Once in the living room, visitors find themselves cantilevered 20 feet over the landscape, eye to eye with the horizon. A six-foot overhang creates shade, making it possible to stare at the view. "Between the front door and the living room, you're choreographed from intimate niches to spectacular views," says architect Mell Lawrence, who was Lamb's partner at the time, and also worked on the house. "It gives the house some mystery."

In the master suite, functions of sleeping and bathing are licentiously mingled. The sink is mounted comfortably close to the fireplace, which in turn warms a dressing room. The bath-tub, as if in perpetual servitude, stretches out near the foot of the bed. The house is full of such unexpected intimacies, visible even in the blueprints; for every powerful event, a private moment occurs. Extra bedrooms are stacked in a 40-foot stone tower, for example, but stair landings on the way up are outfitted with bay windows and telephones. Ultimately, says Lamb, "the house is less about rooms than about places to pause."

Far left: Walls of the five-sided chamber are dressed in polished limestone, cut so neatly that the masons proudly initialed some blocks. Perry Lorenz found the frothy Spanish iron chandelier; its crown of molding was added later. Sheridan had the ceiling painted with a checkerboard—a farmhouse pattern that looked almost Moorish when applied overhead. **Left:** The view from the entry hall, where a 1930s Javanese bench and a Mexican candelabrum share a handwrought heritage. From here, the hall turns right, then decants visitors into the little limestone room.

WHAT THE PROS KNOW ABOUT
CONCRETE FLOORS

Just before the Lorenzes' concrete floors were troweled for the last time, architect Paul Lamb sprinkled on rock salt. Where it dissolved, the floor resembled old, pockmarked stone. "Concrete is highly adaptable," says Lamb. Mixing and troweling are jobs for a contractor, but homeowners can request special effects before, during, or after a floor is poured. *Before:* Have integral color mixed into the concrete. (Frank Lloyd Wright favored terra-cotta red.) Ask to see samples first —though Lamb, who likes earth tones and greens, warns: "You won't know the true color until it dries." *During:* Make fossils with leaves; pat flat without pressing, and let dry. Or seed wet concrete with small pebbles; when dry, smooth with a terrazzo grinder for a terrazzo look. *After:* Apply colored wax (made for the purpose) in tan or light brown, which counteracts the blue-gray undertones of natural concrete. On kitchen floors, use sealer instead to guard against stains.

Far left, top: In the master suite, Sheridan keyed paint colors to travertine tiles around the tub, including sage dressing-room walls (Benjamin Moore's HC-108) and the fawn-colored hearth (Pittsburgh Paint's Lido Beige). **Far left, below:** A tub was planted, like furniture, near the bed. **Left:** In a private corner for washing up, the base of a sink was painted Aegean blue. Lawrence carved away the base of medicine-cabinet doors (at right), creating a miniature Moorish arch.

TUSCAN SPIRIT, TEXAN GOLD

No one knows why, but when you step into a room whose length is 1.618 times greater than the width, you want to stay there. Something about the harmonious shape seems inexplicably perfect—as it did to the Greeks, who calculated it into the Parthenon, and to Palladio, who built it into his villas. Known for centuries as the golden rectangle, its power is just as strong today in Austin—where architect Paul Lamb has built a house that belongs half to Texas and half to 16th-century Tuscany.

The living room is a golden rectangle. Its transomed French doors add up to two golden rectangles, stacked, and even the 16-foot ceiling height is plugged into this ancient ratio (also called the divine proportion). "The room isn't grand," says Lamb, whose prize drafting tool, not surprisingly, is his calculator. "But it is ennobling."

As the clients put it, they wanted their new home to feel like a centuries-old Italian monastery that had been converted to a villa: its architecture lofty but stark, its furnishings luxurious yet slightly sparse. The interior design, by the New Orleans firm Holden & Dupuy, is as intuitive as Lamb's architecture is precise. Rich materials, like an Oushak rug and reedy French

Right: In the living room, an 18th-century daybed, at right, consorts with a new George Smith sofa. New Orleans drapery designer Mary Tait stenciled Italian motifs in silver and gold on the Venetian velvet pillows; the Bayou coffee table is from Holden & Dupuy's Big Easy furniture collection.

Opposite: A French daybed divides a long living room into two conversation areas, and serves both. **Above:** In a subtle shift, architect Paul Lamb moved the Regency X design from the living-room transoms (see opposite) to the bottom of the porch screens, at right. The wall is native limestone.

WHAT THE PROS KNOW ABOUT
SISAL RUGS

On one side of the living room lies a valuable Turkish rug; on the other, a humble carpet of apple-rush matting. Natural fiber flooring, first used by the ancient Egyptians, not only wears well but goes with everything. Sisal, coarse and highly textured, is the best-known vegetable fiber; its cousins are coir, jute, sea grass, abaca (kin to banana plants), and rush, or hollow reeds. Prices vary sharply: depending on where and how smoothly the fiber is spun, and whether or not it has a latex backing to keep dirt from sifting through, a 9-by-12 coir rug can range in price from $99 to $999. If you go barefoot, consider jute (too soft for high-traffic use). On stairs, be wary of loosely woven sisal or coir—high heels may catch—and slippery sea grass. Consider sea grass for family rooms, however, because of its better stain resistance. In bathrooms, stick with rush, which tolerates humidity.

daybed, help bring the living room down to a human scale; so does warm, incandescent lighting. Armchairs draw visitors right up to the hearth. Though the room measures 30 feet long, says designer Ann Dupuy: "It's a sensual, enveloping space."

If the inspiration was Italian, however, the structure of this house is plainly Texan. Limestone for the exterior walls and master bathroom was locally quarried and smeared with mortar—a regional technique that lets a builder use inexpensive rubble stone and still attain a unified surface. Indoors, the floors are laid with wide, salvaged pine planks, typical of early Texan homes, and the deep overhangs are a typically Southern defense against the sun.

The easy bond between Palladian proportions and Texan sensibilities was not merely a confluence of good ideas. Instead, Lamb traces it to a series of discussions between architect and designers that began, unusually enough, before the house was even sketched. "We talked about the nuances, the finishes, the quality of light," he recalls. With this rare collaboration, the interior decoration was not patted on at the end, but bred in the bone.

Opposite: The library measures 20 feet in every dimension. "It feels fantastic to stand in a cube," explains Lamb. "Your hair kind of stands up." The bas relief looks carved, but is inexpensively cast in plaster, and the hearth strategically half blocks the windows so a neighbor's house vanishes from view. Bookshelves are scooped out of the wall for an architecturally massive look. **Left:** An antique Italian sideboard in the living room holds a lamp fashioned from a curvaceous Italian candlestick. French doors to a narrow terrace are reflected in the silver-leaf mirror. **Below left:** Instead of one entry door, this house has a bank of five French doors that open onto the garden terrace; as a result, this long gallery doubles as voluminous foyer and dining room. **Below:** The arched overdoor ornament—one of a pair in the dining gallery—is an Irish antique, but pilasters are newly faux-painted to match.

Left: In the master bath, mirrors, cut to the same golden proportions as the windows, multiply the lake views. Lamb sequestered the shower and water closet in mirrored private compartments. **Top:** Puddled silk drapery around the bed defines a private space within the master bedroom; appliqué in an Italianate serpentine design loops around the canopy. **Above:** A Fortuny-style chandelier from Venice hangs in the living room. The cypress ceiling beams above it are milled from logs that a salvager hauled from the Louisiana bayous.

SOUTH

THESE HOMES, THE BEST OF THE SOUTH,
TAKE A GRACEFUL BOW TO HISTORY YET
RETAIN THEIR MODERN EDGE

137

BUILDING ON HISTORY, COURTING THE BREEZE

Like the best new southern houses, this one, in Windsor, Florida, embraces an old heritage: it adapts itself to natural breezes, not just to central air. Its architects, Andres Duany and Elizabeth Plater-Zyberk, strung 4,000 square feet into a one-room-deep house that wraps itself around three sides of a courtyard. As a result, every room channels the wind. Says Duany, "Cross-ventilation reminds people what it's like to have a breeze through an open casement window with the curtains fluttering."

Duany and Plater-Zyberk are best known as urban planners who design new towns, from Windsor, near Palm Beach, to the celebrated Seaside. To give this model home an instant past, they borrowed one—largely from the historic Florida town of St. Augustine. There, the Spanish enfolded courtyards with masonry houses; the English, coming later, added second stories of wood with long, graceful porches off the bedrooms. The hybrid style, centuries old, gives this house its deep connection to outdoor life.

No foyer was necessary: the front door opens into a porte cochere, or sheltered breezeway, to the courtyard. From there, French doors give access to every room; the trip from living room to master bedroom can only be made outdoors, under a covered loggia. "The house manipulates you."

Above right: A low bridge arches across one end of the 40-foot pool; it connects the loggia, at left, to the garden.
Right and far right: A 70-foot-long porch runs along the second-floor. Climbing vines add definition to the base of the house; they are trimmed to grow no higher.

Left: Interior designer Susan Schuyler Smith, who designed the interior, painted the ground-floor master bedroom robin's-egg blue to evoke a porch ceiling. Draperies of loosely woven linen, a fabric used in every room for unity and simplicity, hang in the doorway to the loggia. **Right:** Smith recalled plantation homes in Jamaica when she furnished the family room. She gave the walls a yellow wash and chose light, natural materials: rattan furniture, sky-blue upholstery, a cotton and sisal rug. **Below right:** Bed hangings in the master bedroom are sheer linen, like the lightweight draperies. Curtain rods, as in every room, are faux bamboo. A 19th-century English bench awaits blankets at the foot of the bed.

WHAT THE PROS KNOW ABOUT
INTEGRATING A POOL
WITH THE HOUSE

To you, it's cool relief from the hot sun, a private place to swim. To your architect, it's a design element that must complement the house. "A pool should never be thoughtlessly placed," says Xavier Iglesias, an architect with Duany Plater-Zyberk. The urban-planning firm has two strategies for siting a pool: either close to the house, so it works as an outdoor room; or tucked deep in the garden, where landscaping provides a sense of enclosure. Either way, a swimmer should emerge from the water into a space that feels defined, not stranded in the middle of a lawn. Be conscious, too, of what the pool reflects. This is not just a matter of placement, says Iglesias, but of the paint inside the pool. The darker the interior, the more mirrorlike the water—and the more natural the pool will look. He has used black paint (which often, in his experience, turns blue) and navy; in this case, the pool is painted the grayish blue of a darkening sky.

GETTING WHITE
RIGHT IN
THE BIG EASY

Eventually, the curtains will have to go. A long pour of white, loose-weave linen—machine-washed, sun-dried, and hung with wrinkles intact—they will ultimately succumb to the glare of New Orleans daylight and start to yellow. No matter, say the designers, Ann Holden and Ann Dupuy. An unlined slip of linen is simple to replace—and what else could offer so sensuous a filter for the sun?

The house, built in well-heeled, uptown New Orleans for a couple in the fashion business, has the Palladian symmetry and the grand simplicity of an Italian villa. And, like every Holden and Dupuy interior, it has been painted, glazed, whitewashed, draped, and upholstered in at least a dozen colors—all of them off-white.

There is the Cafe au Lait bench from the designers' own Big Easy collection, tautly jacketed in creamy tan leather. There is the sofa, wearing its vanilla linen slipcover like a summer frock. Curtain rods are pickled, so their wood grain shows through a wash of white paint, and the dining-room walls have been glazed for translucency—in three shades of white, starting with

Right: Even the most sculptural objects in the living room —side tables balanced on iron arrows, and the Noguchi lamp—serve a purpose, which gives the space visual intrigue without clutter. The Gumbo Ya Ya armchairs are from the designers' Big Easy furniture collection, as is the wooden table with distressed gilt; the 1930s photograph is by Fonville Winans.

the palest. Without such a mix of textures and hues, Dupuy points out, no monochromatic room could keep the senses engaged.

Small shots of color are occasionally admitted, partly because they help to animate all that white. (As does sunlight; hence the wisp of linen at the windows.) Wood is cultivated for its dark, almost historic gleam. Touches of gold are encouraged, though in small measure. Books and gardens alone provide what the two Anns, as their clients call them, consider "natural color." Indeed, some of the most intriguing tension of these rooms comes from some of the smallest contrasts—like a slipcover's kick pleat that reveals a lining of white-on-white striped fabric. Says Dupuy, in all seriousness: "That's the accent color."

Though the first floor has only three main rooms (living, dining, and open kitchen), everything has been carried out on a scale that is slightly larger than life. French doors to the garden nearly touch the 10-foot ceiling, and furnishings, both new and antique, are strapping in size. The fawn-colored cement floor, poured by architect Val Dansereau in lieu of limestone, is scored in 30-inch squares to suggest extra-large stone slabs. Dansereau also gave the living room its massive ceiling beams. "Overscaled is always better," says Dupuy. "It speaks of quality over quantity. Besides, it's more comfortable."

Left: The wet bar, situated near the front door, was designed around an 1830s English pub bar. A wooden *santo,* reigning from a pedestal, was carved in Mexico. **Right:** The placement was almost impertinent—a table with three plaster feet, designed by John Dickenson in the 1960s, attending an 18th-century Venetian settee in the living room. The settee's new, tabbed upholstery is typical of its period. **Far right:** A chandelier dangles like an earring over the dining room. Slipcovers and tablecloth are of the same linen, a rare instance where fabrics were matched; white glazes were hand-brushed on the walls for the subtle texture of strié-like brush strokes. The photographs are by Helmut Newton.

WHAT THE PROS KNOW ABOUT
WORKING WITH WHITE

A Holden and Dupuy white room follows easy-to-adapt rules. The designers use only one paint finish—eggshell or semigloss—on ceiling, walls, and trim. Reserve pure white for fabrics; choose a warmer off-white, like Benjamin Moore's Linen White, for walls. Try other shades on ceilings and moldings, like Moore's Navajo White and China White, but test each where you plan to use it: White reflects the colors of floors and furnishings nearby. Glazing walls white makes a room luminous. (Prime the walls white first.) And remember that white includes a range from ivory to beige.

MAMEY, MANGO, AND THE MIAMI VERNACULAR

Chunky and gray, cinder block is the architectural currency of modern Miami. Humidity can't damage it. Insects can't colonize it. The lime rock used in these concrete blocks lies directly underground—giving easy access, which lowers the cost. And cinder block dresses up easily with a coat of painted stucco.

But Jorge Trelles and Mari Tere Cabarrocas-Trelles, married partners in Trelles Architects, opted for honesty: building their suburban home just across Biscayne Bay from Miami, they left key sections of concrete and cinder block exposed. A concrete ceiling the color of storm clouds seems to float over the living room; columns along the terrace are massive stacks of cinder block. "It's a raw material, the vernacular of Miami," says Jorge.

Designed by Jorge and Luis Trelles, his older brother (and the firm's third partner), the house is elsewhere painted in colors that remind them of their native Cuba and of island hues seen throughout Miami. Many of its rooms and courtyard walls are color-matched to tropical fruits: the yellow and dark red of a ripe mango, the coral red of mamey. "The colors are particular to the light of Miami," says Jorge. "They are not decoration, but architecture."

Right: The nine-foot-tall front door, made of mahogany, opens directly into the living room. **Far right, top:** A sugar-cane motif is cut into a balcony railing off the second-floor loggia. **Far right, below:** The front door is reached through an entry court. Colorist Emilio Cianfoni stirred lime into the exterior paint to invite weathering.

Right: The wall of an interior courtyard, just off the living room, is painted the color of mamey, a tropical fruit. **Far right, top:** A 16-foot-deep verandah, furnished like an indoor room, is bordered at right by cinder block columns. Floorboards are recycled Dade County pine. **Far right, below:** The loggia is exposed to breezes on three sides and provides a kind of natural air-conditioning for the second floor. Its floor is waxed concrete applied with a steel trowel for a silky surface.

WHAT THE PROS KNOW ABOUT
TROPICAL COLORS

Architect Jorge Trelles keys the coloration of a house strictly to its natural surroundings. Does this mean a native Chicagoan can't have a shot of Cuban color, at least indoors? Not at all: the trick lies in muting or brightening the hues to suit the natural light. "A tropical palette should be several octaves lower in the North, where the sun is less intense," says Kenneth X. Charbonneau, a color marketing consultant for Benjamin Moore & Co. Look at the room itself, he adds, not just at the map; a New York room with direct southern exposure will tolerate more saturated colors. For *Metropolitan Home*, Charbonneau devised two variations on the tropical theme, both using Benjamin Moore paints:

Mamey (scarlet): *southern,* no. 1321; *northern,* no. 1300.

Cuban ocher: *southern,* no. 195; *northern,* no. 194.

Mosaic blue: *southern,* no. 818; *northern,* no. 811.

Carib turquoise: *southern,* no. 647; *northern,* no. 641.

Mango: *southern,* no. 307; *northern,* no. 306

Concrete: *southern,* no. 1614; *northern,* no. 1613.

Why the concrete gray? Like cinder block in Trelles's house, it grounds the hotter hues.

Northern Palette
Southern Palette

Left: The master suite was built entirely of wood, inside and out, to commemorate the cabins built by early Florida pioneers. Wood was as ubiquitous then as cinder block is today; by using both, Jorge Trelles made the house appear both modern and historic. The bedroom ceiling has a rooflike slant; the louvered closet door suggests a plantation shutter. Local artisan David D'Imperio made the curved chest veneered with African wood.

Above: Accessories throughout the house—like the Italian glass lamp at bedside—are kept simple, with little ornament to distract the eye. **Right:** Sheer bed curtains evoke an easy tropical mood without resorting to the cliché of mosquito netting. Paint on the bedroom walls was matched to the yellowest part of an avocado; outside, the bedroom "cabin" is painted avocado green.

MID-
ATLANTIC

THEIR BONES MAY BE BAUHAUS OR
PUREBRED COLONIAL, BUT THESE HOUSES
ARE FURNISHED WITH CONTRASTS, NOT
COMPLEMENTS—AS HOMES, NOT MUSEUMS

153

SPANNING CENTURIES: AN ECONOMY OF STYLE

The house is a Bauhaus-style sugar cube, all rigor and restraint. Built in 1931 by a daring architect, it must have rattled the neighbors in Bucks County, Pennsylvania—a constellation of farms, Amish communities, and pleasantly dusty antique shops. Yet in this stark period piece of a house, where one might expect to find chairs by Le Corbusier and Mies van der Rohe, rooms are seeded with 18th- and 19th-century furnishings.

The antiques, as stripped of ornament as the house, seem to belong here. "We knew we'd furnish the place true to period—but period Americana," says David Guilmet, an interior designer who lives here with design partner and antiques dealer Patrick Bell. "Our furniture has straightforward lines and a utilitarian comfort that fit the Bauhaus philosophy."

The house had retained its original boxy rooms, and on closing day, Guilmet armed himself with a sledgehammer and gouged out walls, cabinets, and the second-story ceiling, just six and a half feet high. Three bedrooms became one. The breakfast and living rooms merged. And a new sliver of a window, 14 feet high and just 12 inches wide, funnels light over the stairs.

To their angular home, the designers added two sinuous, and well-calculated, swerves. The first, outside, is a rounded wall that conceals a vest-pocket patio; it holds a fountain in its half-moon embrace. The second, indoors, is a cat's-tail curve at the base of the stairs, which had been pencil straight. Now the steps flare into the living room, entrancing the eye. "Bauhaus can be rigid," says Guilmet. "The curves give it a touch of movement."

The rest of the house repeats a grid pattern that the designers picked up from the panes of

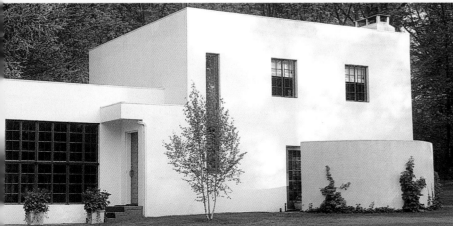

Above: On the living-room wall—its new curve lit from above by wall-washers—hangs an abstract watercolor the same vintage as the house. In a rare burst of color, an 1820s painted chest meets a 1930s Heriz rug. Stairs are clad in black slate. **Left:** The house after renovation, with a new curved wall that conceals a tiny living-room patio, and a stainless-steel front door. The lawn was cleared, making the grass part of a geometric composition.

Above: The kitchen, still unrenovated, has a new floor of peel-and-stick sisal squares (easily replaced if stained), and a mid-19th-century chopping table. **Right:** In the living room, the curves of a piano and Windsor chair underscore the geometry of the windows and shelves. **Opposite:** Dining-room walls are covered in taupe velvet, tactile but neutral. The fabric was given a paper backing and glued up like wallpaper.

the casement windows. Their new dining-room floor, for example, is a geometric inlay of cherry and Pennsylvania black slate. A bedroom storage unit, salvaged from the dining room and silver-leafed, is a graphic compilation of little drawers and doors.

The designers tested 22 shades of white before mixing one that stays gallery-white all day, resisting reflections of the grass and sky. Neutral fabrics render the upholstered pieces half invisible, ceding center stage to the antiques.

In this spare setting, timeworn furnishings seem to have drifted into small groupings, seeking solitude and light. "With all the clean lines and polished floors and black slate," says Bell, "everything you put into these rooms becomes a focal point."

WHAT THE PROS KNOW ABOUT
METAL LEAF

What looks like silver leaf on Bell and Guilmet's cabinetry (left) is in fact composition leaf, persuasively faked with aluminum. Composition leaf, also called Dutch metal, is easier to work with, and cheaper than the real thing. (You might pay $5.60 for a book of 25 leaves, or 5½-inch squares, of composition metal; $9 for real silver; and $22 for 22-karat gold.) Guilmet's five tips for beginners: Try oil gilding, which is easier than water gilding. Start with a small, horizontal surface, like a table-top. To age the tinfoil brightness of new leaf, apply asphaltum (wipe off excess with a rag dipped in naphtha). Don't strive for perfection—small flaws add to the antiqued look. And don't start any project without recipelike instructions. A catalog of leaf, books, and project kits is available from Baggot Leaf Co. in New York (212.431.4653).

Opposite and below: In the master bedroom, a 1930s storage unit—originally built into the dining room—was hauled upstairs in pieces, reconfigured to hold the television, and refinished with composition silver leaf.
Above: The bed wears a quilted cotton suit in beige, to match the rug; as a result, a visitor's attention goes straight to the art and furnishings, including a leggy, 18th-century Black Forest chair.

AN UPDATED FARMHOUSE HINTS AT THE PAST

The farmer who built this house, back in 1910 or so, placed it where it made the most sense: right near his fields. But when Charles Bohl, an architect, and his wife, Barbara, an interior designer, bought the 75-acre spread, they hauled the house to a new spot 100 yards away, where red cedars towered on either side and the Chesapeake Bay shimmered out back.

The house is a classic American foursquare: four rooms, one in each corner, on each floor. In the farmer's day, one could order it, in parts, from Sears Roebuck, and it became a familiar form in many parts of the country. But Chip Bohl reworked the structure, styling its columns and cornerstones after the Greek Revival farmhouses along Maryland's Eastern Shore. In the process, he combined rooms and stripped off or omitted some finished surfaces, indoors and out—a Bohl design trademark that alludes to erosion and ruins.

Thus the new front porch, where an empty skylight, a simple cutout, appears to have long since lost its glass, and where the columns—cedar planks with gaps between them—look like structural bones from which stucco has crumbled away. The porch floor's freshly painted

Right: Chip Bohl designed the new front porch to suggest the half-ruined shell of a Doric temple. At its center is a late-19th-century garden urn. **Far right, top:** The farmland in front of the house has been planted with sunflowers, which are echoed by yellow trim on the house. **Far right, below:** A wooden path, wide enough for two, hugs the slope between the garage and the front porch.

Left: Chip and Barbara Bohl merged two square rooms at the rear of the house to form the great room, with new French doors placed centrally and flanked with glass inserts. The massive-looking door surround is made of marine-grade plywood, but the Bohls created the texture of rough limestone by stirring sand into the paint.

WHAT THE PROS KNOW ABOUT
PAINTED FLOORS

Rather than using pattern as a painted carpet, Chip and Barbara Bohl saw it as a carpet *border*—with the bare floorboards serving as a rug. This let them "zone" the great room into three areas, each outlined by a Greek key design, making it easy to site furniture. The room's most prominent feature—the square columns of the door surround—established the border's hefty size. (Large rooms with high ceilings require a bigger design.) Several steps simplify the painting process, according to the Bohls:

- Hire a professional to lightly sand the floor first, so no old varnish remains.

- Use the width of a floorboard to set the width of a painted line. If this means that the design is two inches closer to the wall on one side of the room, so be it.

- Paint the entire area with the lightest color first—in this case, gray; for a classic checkerboard, white.

- Draw the lines first with pencil, but don't mask them off with tape. Slight imprecision adds to the sense of artisanship.

- Use one coat of paint, followed by several coats of polyurethane. In high-traffic areas, the Bohls prefer oil-based products.

design was left unsealed, to be worn away by foot traffic and rain. And in the most jolting reference to architecture that has fallen away, in parts, over time, Chip sliced out floor-to-ceiling strips of the great-room walls, inserting sheets of glass in their place. Lacking sills and woodwork, these glass panels read as shockingly empty space, baring the room to the landscape.

Indoors, Barbara painted the rooms in farm colors—barn red, plow yellow, tractor green—borrowed from the agricultural tradition that has thrived in this region for centuries. The palette constructs an instant history for the house, yet makes the place difficult to date. So do the appointments, like the early-20th-century porch lights used throughout the interior, and scarred leather chairs whose patina is proof of a past. "The most comfortable houses have no single moment of construction," says Chip. "They look like they've been built and modified and renovated over a long period of time."

Left: A hobo-art chair, made in the 1920s of shovel handles, faces the front door. **Above:** A classic but oversized Greek key border, painted on the great-room floor, corresponds in scale to a zinc-topped worktable near the kitchen. **Right:** A dining niche, also in the great room, faces the bay through unexpected slices of glass.

Left: Open shelving on simple brackets, and the beaded board paneling behind it, add up to a farmhouse kitchen without pretensions. A student lamp, wired directly into the wall, lights the sink; Chip installed the interior windows so the kitchen and adjacent dining room could share the breeze. **Above:** Window frames in the master bedroom—and throughout the house—are painted an unobtrusive charcoal gray so as not to compete with the view. The room is furnished with art nouveau pieces by Louis Majorelle. **Right:** A janitor's utility sink, with a stainless-steel "curb" along the edge to protect the enamel from mops and blankets, gives a first-floor guest room an industrial edge.

GENTEEL AND UNRETOUCHED: AN APPEARANCE OF CHANCE

Nathaniel Irish designed this Philadelphia town house in 1752 and spent the next ten years building it by hand. A master carpenter, he made his home a showcase: the rooms were unusually large (about 18 feet square) and tall (9½ feet, or 24 inches higher than most) for those pre-Revolutionary days. And, with an artisan's flourish, Irish varied the woodwork from room to room, so he could walk clients through a life-sized sample book.

The two men who live there now—Glen Senk, president of the Anthropologie home-furnishings and clothing stores, and Keith Johnson, its antiques buyer and head of product development—inherited Irish's work intact. To their amazement, no previous owner had ever varnished the pine floorboards, or chiseled off the 18th-century plasterwork, or even changed the knobs on the doors. Even in this historic neighborhood of Queen Village, where the streets retain their cobblestones, an unaltered house is a rare find.

But that doesn't mean they treat it like a museum piece. To antique the dining room paneling, which they painted army green, Senk and Johnson whipped out soft rags and started buffing the walls—with black shoe polish. In their living room, the most prominent pictures are not paintings at all, but blown-up photographs of vintage French puzzles. And furnishings

Right: A late-19th-century dollhouse cabinet hangs in the third-floor master bedroom. In a typical mix of rare and humble objects, Senk's childhood handprint, set in plaster, stands in the top left cubby. Below is a highly collectible Scottish butcher's scale.

Right: The present dining room, on the first floor, was originally a formal salon, while the upstairs living room was once a private gathering spot for intimate friends only. Armchairs are upholstered in mohair, not velvet, for its older, richer feel. **Below:** In the living room, a Louis XVI console table stands behind a lowly metal daybed from a French monastery. **Opposite:** Johnson made the hall cabinet from salvaged wood. He and Senk reproduced the Edwardian mirror, an English shop fixture, for the Anthropologie stores.

were chosen not for pedigree but for their evocative lines. (Some Johnson dug out of a Dumpster and, moved by their weather-beaten looks, cleaned but did not restore them.) As a result, when a true Louis XVI console table takes its place in the house, it adds, without snobbishness, simply its own fine-boned beauty to the mix.

Because the building's four stories are vertically stacked along skinny stairs, few visitors venture higher than the second-floor living room. Here, the furnishings have a worn sort of gentility, and statuary looms up in unexpected spots, like heirlooms that had to go, well, somewhere. But the floor and windows are conspicuously bare, and the space is monochromatic, with pale yellow walls that seem tinged by years of smoke. Even the daybed and coffee table, though surrounded by slightly eccentric objects, are carefully centered. "You may think I'm nuts, but I regard it as a pretty clean-lined room," says Senk. "It makes the house feel very modern and very old at the same time."

WHAT THE PROS KNOW ABOUT
THE ART OF DISPLAY

"When objects are symmetrically placed, the result can be incredibly dull," says Keith Johnson. Instead, he says, an arrangement should appear to have fallen into place by chance—an illusion that actually requires a sense of order. On the living room console, a skyline of old telescopes (at left) has the same visual weight as the shorter, broader drawing at right. Says Johnson, "Balance is not achieved by having similar things on either side." The partners' tips for grouping objects:

- Seek out some contrast in color, texture, or size.

- Find the focal point—here, the tallest telescope—and place it opposite another prominent, but very different, piece.

- Play with the arrangement until your gaze naturally sweeps, in a rough figure eight, from side to side and back. (Step back frequently to gauge your reaction.) A worthy exception: collections of identical objects, like the four mossy flowerpots above the hall cabinet (left), tend to invite closer inspection when lined up like troops.

Above: A cooking fireplace in the never-renovated ground-floor kitchen now holds pottery. The contemporary Viking range looks natural here, says Senk, because of its industrial appearance. **Right:** In the dining room stands a lineup of American Centennial chairs—an early Colonial style reissued in 1876 to celebrate 100 years of American independence. Their look is a marriage of Spanish and Chippendale. Above them, leaning without pretense on top of the wainscoting, are early-20th-century watercolors of Noritake china patterns.

If Palladio had designed a workaday warehouse, it might have looked something like this—clean-lined and classical, despite its humble purpose, with good bones and a stucco facade. In fact, this suburban warehouse was built in 1926 by a group of moonlighting Italian masons who, in their day jobs, were building the Gothic-style Princeton University dorms.

The interior comprised 44 storerooms, unheated and unwired, when the architect Michael Graves spotted it in 1970. Envisioning a Cinderella transformation from furniture storehouse to Tuscan-style villa, Graves bought the L-shaped building for $35,000—a hardship for the then-struggling Princeton professor, not yet famous for launching post-modernism in America. In waves of renovation over the years, an unusual hybrid has evolved: part private home, part design laboratory, and part tourist attraction, with buses disgorging the curious for docent-led tours.

The Warehouse has a processional quality, with small, formal spaces decanting a visitor into larger, higher rooms. To reach his own bath, for example, Graves must walk through a skylit rotunda, heightening the sense of ceremony. And to enter the circular foyer, a visitor first passes through a formal, roomlike courtyard. Taking advantage of his two stacked circular rooms, the rotunda and foyer, Graves topped them with a skylit cupola and channeled a three-story round opening, or oculus, all the way down—giving visitors good reason to crane their necks.

"Most of the rooms are 'centered,'" says Graves, describing the sense of balance that his work embodies. "They're not always symmetrical, but you feel centered in the room." A doorway sited

Left: Guest-room chairs are loosely slipcovered in white, a note of ease not seen in the public rooms. An upholstered Biedermeier daybed is attended by a 19th-century bench that can serve as footrest, coffee table, or extra seat. **Above:** The west wing hall has stonelike walls, made of fiberboard panels applied in a pattern of squares and painted a glossy shade of cream. Winding stairs lead up to the guest-bedroom wing.

Right: A covered terrace connects the east garden to the library. The Warehouse's graveled paths linking gardens, terraces, and entryways. **Below:** The living-room fireplace, with polished black granite mantel, looks doubly massive because of floor-to-ceiling windows that Graves installed on either side. **Opposite:** Removal of a staircase left Graves with a high, narrow space on the ground floor. Now a formal library, its shelving was designed to suggest tall buildings along a miniature street.

midway in the wall, for example, is likely to face a fireplace; windows are balanced by a doorway directy opposite. As a result, says Graves, "You understand a room by your presence in it."

The walls appear ivory, but reward a close examination. "There are four or five shades of white from the baseboard to what we call the lower wall, a kind of wainscot," says Graves. "There's an upper-wall color, a soffit color, and a second soffit color, which is not actually white at all but a terribly light gray-blue." This pale progression begins at the baseboards with the darkest off-white, lifting the ceiling with the lightest hue, and making rooms appear properly weighted.

The house is furnished with Biedermeier pieces, some of which resemble small temples. On mantels, niches, and shelves, the architect's Grand Tour objects—19th-century copies of classical objects, like reproduction Grecian urns—are both exalted and (because they are everywhere) familiar. Books are just as ubiquitous, with towering stacks growing like tall weeds around his bed. In these rooms that are painted by sunlight, Graves lives amid the tools of his inspiration.

WHAT THE PROS KNOW ABOUT
COLLECTING BIEDERMEIER FURNITURE

Michael Graves's first Biedermeier purchase, his round living-room coffee table, is flawed: a onetime Bavarian tea table, it has sawed-down legs. "It lost its value," says Graves, "but it was right for me." Biedermeier furniture—veneered (to keep its cost down for the middle class, its primary market) and adorned with pediments and other neo-classical elements—was made only briefly, in Europe, Russia, and Scandinavia. The most collectible examples are early (1815 to 1835) or unusual (secretaries with elaborate interiors) or small (like wastebaskets), says Niall Smith, owner of Niall Smith Antiques and Decorations in New York. More affordable are the simpler, heavier "late" furnishings (1835 to 1848). Smith's advice: save Biedermeier sofas for secondary seating, as they foster perching, not reclining. And don't reject cracked veneer. "It comes with age," says Smith. "Just enjoy the piece as it is." Few pieces are dated, so age is gauged by eye. A good resource: *Biedermeier,* by Angus Wilkie.

Above: Niches in the master bedroom hold statuary and serve as sources for indirect lighting. The grid of the black metal windows, designed and installed by Graves, is echoed near the niches by a dado (the lower third of a wall) scored to resemble stone. **Right:** Two 19th-century French sinks stand in the master bath. Graves designed the alabaster sconces and chose Verona red marble for the floor because it brought back memories of Italian churches and piazzas. Square mirrors continue the theme of the grid. **Opposite:** Standing lamps in the master bedroom, as elsewhere, are made from Grand Tour candlesticks—early-19th-century copies of ancient Roman originals. For consistency, all wear the same black shades throughout the house.

NEW YORK

NESTLED IN A FORMER LONG ISLAND
POTATO FIELD OR GLITTERING IN THE
CITY SKYLINE, THE WAY HERE IS SUBTLE
SOPHISTICATION AND A SENSE OF RETREAT

181

A DAZZLING BACKDROP FOR ORDER AND ART

Most collectors frame their pictures with museum-white walls. But Nicholas Howey, an abstract artist, and Gerard Widdershoven, a dealer of art deco furnishings, felt no such deference for the contemporary art in their own Manhattan town house. No, the house itself had to join their collection, they told interior designer Carl D'Aquino. It had to engage with the art and set a brilliant stage for all those dark and finely drawn art deco chairs.

The house was designed as a private home in 1858 by the architect James Renwick, who gave it fine bones, high ceilings, and narrow rooms strung like pearls around a curving stair. It had sunk to the status of rooming house over the years, so D'Aquino began a surgical restoration—realigning doorways, prying out wallboard, vanquishing the cubbyhole esthetic of boardinghouse life.

Visitors now enter a red vestibule, then are drawn through a pumpkin foyer and living room, cobalt dining room, emerald kitchen and guest room, paper-bag-tan bedroom, and, in the master bath at the top of the house, a parting shot of red. The progression of colors creates a sense of order, and because the house offers so many moods, it appears larger than its 1,200 square feet. As for the central staircase, D'Aquino made it a kaleidoscopic sculpture, covering its steps with patterned remnants of movie-theater carpeting. "I see the stairs as a refreshing sorbet, the cleansing course between rooms of different color," says D'Aquino. "It acts as the spine of the house, and it gives tremendous strength."

Above: In the living room, under a blazing painting by Donna Moylan, is a gathering of refined 20th-century classics: a Josef Hoffmann table (far left), angular Francis Jourdain armchair, and Bruno Paul rug. **Far left:** To create the stormy dining room walls, Nicholas Howey rolled blue theatrical acrylic paint over a base coat of white latex paint, then quickly rubbed it with cheesecloth before it could dry. French 1920s chairs are by Louis Majorelle. **Left:** Stairway walls are painted the palest yellow—the only temperate color in the house—to let the carpet remnants stand out.

A VILLA ABOVE THE URBAN SPRAWL

Laurence and William Kriegel live in a 6,000-square-foot French villa that just happens to be at the top of a former chocolate factory, high above the trendy art galleries of SoHo. Its carved and battered doors, salvaged from old châteaux, swing from 19th-century hinges. Its floors are laid with barn boards and with ruddy terra-cotta tiles pried from a Provençal estate. Even the water music you hear is played by an antiquated stone fountain from the south of France.

"I believe in the beauty of the materials," says Laurence, who shopped salvage yards in France to supply her home (and to stock her Wooster Street shop, Intérieurs). As a result, the Kriegels hung few paintings on their hand-polished plaster walls, and unfurled no rugs. "I wanted it pure," explains Laurence. "When the floors creak, I feel like I am on vacation."

The villa, designed by architects Edward Asfour and Peter Guzy, occupies the building's top floor and two-tiered roof. Visitors enter through a lacy iron gate, and are drawn through rooms that Asfour and Guzy arrayed in the old European style—around a central court, or interior terrace. A gardenlike room, the court is flooded by sun from its glass ceiling.

The living room's massive hearth, built entirely of old brick, consumes an entire wall. Its proportions were adapted from the Kriegels' other home, an annex to a 16th-century castle in

Right: Laurence Kriegel set up a time warp in the entrance to the loft: to step past the foyer, visitors push open a 19th-century iron gate and confront a contemporary painting by Canadian artist Michel Pellus.

France. The kitchen, with double doors set into a solid wall of cabinetry, can seat 16 for dinner.

Even the walls appear to be imported from a grander and older place. It took a long time to find plasterers who understood imperfection—a state of grace, for the Kriegels, in which the touch of the artisan's hand comes through. The finish on the walls, rarely seen in this country, is *lustro veneziano,* a lost art of the trowel in which whisper-thin layers of plaster are tinted with pigments and slowly built up until the surface is smooth as wax. In places, the walls are 14 inches thick; Laurence, standing in the kitchen, knows it is pointless to call out to her children.

Yet the city asserts an industrial, almost gritty presence in the space. A zinc duct races across the living-room ceiling; no effort was made to conceal it. The steel fire door, commissioned to hide the

Left: New rafters of salvaged wood were installed in the living-room ceiling. The library table was rescued from an old shirt store in the south of France. **Above:** The foyer's wrought-iron gate, also found in France. Stairs were built of salvaged barn boards. **Above center:** Thresholds are marked by small riverbeds of smooth, white pebbles that were prodded into wet concrete and left to set. **Above right:** Near the living room's fire door, a 19th-century wire model of the Eiffel Tower.

freight elevator, is indigenous to New York factory lofts. The rooftop's defunct water tank was preserved as an urban icon; Laurence holds intimate lunches in its round, cedar-scented interior.

And baseboards in many rooms are lanky bands of steel—a reminder that even where old-world plaster meets honeyed floorboards, this loft remains rooted in Manhattan.

"It really feels like a villa," says Guzy, who, like Asfour, has lived and worked in Europe. "But this is not some replication of a Provençal fantasy. This is something newly arrived at. We wanted to evoke the serene quality of Provençal architecture—and combine it with an esthetic that never forgets it's in New York."

Above left: Doors between the kitchen and the court were discovered in another section of the loft, carved into a new arched shape, and reinstalled with 19th-century French iron hardware. **Above:** The kitchen, with appliances and cabinetry by La Cornue, has a pot-filler faucet over the stove. **Right:** The court, sunlit by a glass ceiling, opens into the foyer, kitchen, and living room; the arched window funnels light into a rear hallway. Laurence Kriegel found the 18th-century rocker in France.

WHAT THE PROS KNOW ABOUT
STONE SINKS

Laurence Kriegel's stone sink was assembled from French limestone slabs, sealed and set in a base of reclaimed pine. More common is soapstone, popular in the 19th century because it kept boiled water warm for hours. This gray stone resists even red-wine stains, says Glenn Bowman, owner of the Vermont Soapstone Company (800.284.5404), where most sinks run $800 to $1,200. Hand-chiseled granite sinks—rough-hewn bowls (for the bath) or rectangular basins (for kitchen use)—run $900 to $2,500 at Alan Court & Associates in East Hampton, New York (516.324.7497). Alternatively, call a stone quarry: a mason might take on a custom job.

Opposite: Walls in the master bath slope inward, teepee-style, because the entire room was built inside the slanting supports of the old water tank on the roof. The architects compared it to "building underneath the Eiffel Tower, but on a very small scale." The sink was custom-made of French limestone in the shape of a trough; the tub was cast of dusky-plum-colored cement. The diamond-shaped opening is an air-conditioning vent. **Above left:** Beneath the water tank, the bathroom's arched glass doors open onto the rooftop's landscaped terrace. **Above:** A wooden screen behind the bathroom sink shields a dressing area on the left, a shower directly in back, and a water closet on the right. Its mirrors reflect the window above the tub.

Far left: Though the worn floorboards suggest otherwise, the master bedroom was newly constructed on the roof. It is cooled by a vintage fan, and lit by bulbs that dangle like earrings over the bed. The hand-painted silk lights are Venetian. **Left:** The architects fashioned bedroom shutters from leftover wide-plank floorboards. They cut tiny florets into the wood, a technique they borrowed from Swiss farmhouses; the florets are not only decorative but serve to focus sunbeams on the floor with laser-like intensity.

WHAT THE PROS KNOW ABOUT
WORKING WITH
ARCHITECTURAL SALVAGE

Salvage gives a room instant history—but only after it's been coaxed to work or fit. The Kriegels' antique French doors demanded custom-carved doorways; their floorboards, pulled up from old barns, had to be kiln-dried and machined to a uniform thickness. Work only with experts on salvage, advises Peter Guzy, as an overzealous contractor can polish the patina out of vintage materials. Lessons from the loft: Recycle extra floorboards as radiator grilles, stairs, or shutters. For lighting fixtures, invest in new, trustworthy wiring; some shops stock vintage-look cords and plugs. Never buy a door that has warped, or cupped. (The test: does a yardstick lie flat against it?) And don't snap up vintage doorknobs on impulse. The spindle of the knob you're buying must perfectly match the one that's being replaced.

SPARTAN AND SENSUAL: A BOOK-LINED CITY HAVEN

The color on the walls of Michael Hampton's Manhattan apartment is indefinable, which may account for its restfulness. Pittsburgh Paint, in a bit of a reach, calls it Aluminum. It goes white in direct sunlight, green in the late afternoon. At moments, it's the color of concrete. Asked to describe the hue, Hampton, creative director at an advertising agency, says simply: "Peaceful."

Except for one requirement—that his black leather sofa remain—"peaceful" was about the only dictate that Hampton gave his interior designers, Laura Bohn and Joseph Lembo. Their job was to create an airy haven by merging a studio apartment (now the master bedroom) with the choppy two-bedroom next door. This seamless marriage was brought about by the removal of every extraneous wall, and the raising of every doorway to ceiling height. "It lets the ceiling run through the interior views," says Bohn. Windows look bare when the blinds are up, creating steely frames for the gritty Hudson River vista. Carpeting in an unnameable gray-taupe completes this architectural envelope.

For visual intrigue, Lembo and Bohn infused the smallest details with pattern and texture. There is the channel quilting on the white linen wrappers worn by two Mies van der Rohe MR cantilevered chairs. ("Purists would cringe," says Bohn, "but it softens the chairs.") In the

Right: The living-room coffee table is an antique Japanese altar table, its low profile a reiteration of the linear sofa. Behind the Andrée Putman light hangs a portrait by German photographer Heinrich Keuhn.

bedroom, a velvet cushion rests unexpectedly on a battered wicker chair. And even the living room's cedar shelves, rubbed with a wash of Aluminum paint, were first soaked in water for days to raise the grain, making it more prominent.

Color, too, throbs in quiet corners. That black leather sofa now has a slipcover of brittle chartreuse; on it glows a pillow in handpainted Fortuny fabric. The black-and-white photographs that Hampton collects yield luminous grays. In the study, an antique frame leans empty against the wall, its gleaming gilt the real display. "It's an incredibly neutral apartment," says Lembo. "But that's precisely what makes its colors sharp."

Left: In the master bedroom, cast-iron seats from 19th-century threshing machines cast lacy shadows on the wall. **Above:** A living-room side table was sliced from a 10-foot-tall column; a light, planted inside, is diffused by Plexiglas. The cabinet at left separates living and dining areas, and holds a television inside.

WHAT THE PROS KNOW ABOUT
BUILT-IN BOOKCASES

The tailored look of Michael Hampton's book-lined apartment results partly from shelving that was custom-fitted from floor to ceiling and recessed into the walls. For stature, designers Laura Bohn and Joe Lembo made the shelves a generous 17 inches deep; in the living room, for visual softness, they added $1\frac{1}{2}$-inch bullnose edging. Clamp-on lights can be moved around as needed. "We like to mix laminate, which is very practical, with wood, for warmth," says Bohn. "We may do the top of a shelf in laminate so books slide easily off, and the bullnose edge in rough-cut cedar or oak." No supports are visible; the hollow shelves, made of plywood, slip over steel rods that attach to the wall for a look that is clean-lined and architectural. "Even if you paint these pieces a different color from the wall," says Bohn, "they are still a part of the backdrop."

Above left: In a reading corner of the living room, an art deco chair, voluptuous as a Botero sculpture, was propelled further into luxury by its bullion fringe. Clamp-on lights illuminate the shelves. **Left:** In the study, a Walker Evans photograph, circa 1935, is propped up, allowing this important work to feel accessible. The desk chair by Ettore Sottsass provides the room's only curves.
Opposite: The study's built-in banquette, a place to read or put up overnight guests, also hides heating elements. Its end table is a late-19th-century suitcase.

RESTORED BY LIGHT AND AN ARTIST'S TOUCH

Potatoes thrive in cellarlike gloom, and this Bridgehampton, Long Island, barn, built in the 1920s, sheltered a local farmer's crop for years. But the darkness did not discourage Karl Mann, a New York sculptor who perceived, in the barn's cavernous reaches, the makings of a studio and home. Space, his first requirement, stretched out in all directions: the barn is 100 feet long and 40 feet wide, with a 22-foot-high peak. Light, his second necessity, could be surgically admitted through windows, dormers, and tall French doors, none of them preexisting.

There was no wiring, no plumbing. "All I was buying was square footage with a bad roof," says Mann. But the possibilities were irresistible. A neighbor's flower farm would make a lavish view. There was room under the rafters for a second floor. And in its utilitarian, shingle-style frame and its lofty wooden trusses, the barn offered a sense of history that the sculptor and his partner, artist Hector Leonardi, deeply valued. "Even in decorating," says Mann, "if you honor the past, you draw strength from it."

Working with New York architect Robert Ascione, Mann left the front half of the barn at its original height and sited two studios here. Double-height windows saturate the rooms with light;

Top right: A rear view of the barn, with two double-height studios at right, behind the tallest windows. **Right:** In a studio that doubles as a downstairs living room, lanky 1950s chairs mix with antique wicker. A primitive Swedish carved bird stands sentry on a cabinet that Mann made.

like all the barn's new windows, they were assembled from money-saving catalog parts, no custom work required. "We used stock sizes as our vocabulary," says Ascione, who mixed rectangles, triangles, ovals, and rounds. Plate glass might have made the studios brighter, but in a mark of respect to the early-20th-century structure, all the new windows have multiple panes.

Ascione placed a loftlike second floor above the crossties in the back half of the barn. Because the space below had once been furnished with potato bins, Mann wanted a staircase that would glorify the descent. "But I didn't want to make it Baroque or baronial using traditional materials—that would be pretentious in a barn," he says. Instead, he made the railings from the cast-iron frames of antique garden benches, pieces he shipped back from a recent trip to Ireland with no particular use in mind. In the walls, he imbedded dozens of antique blue-and-white platters, also acquired in Ireland.

"I would have hung them," says Mann, "but because my house is a barn, it seemed important to make a statement that I was committed to it. Sinking the platters into the wall was like saying, 'This is permanent.' You might not figure it out, but you sense it, unconsciously. This is home."

Far left: The dining room, along with the kitchen and other daytime rooms, was sited on the second floor, where sunlight is most plentiful. The harvest table is ringed by Mann's characteristic mix of chairs; the cabinets in back have doors fashioned from shoji screens that the sculptor bought in Japan. To break up the 50-foot expanse of the new second story, floorboards were laid on the diagonal. **Left:** Mann rewelded the frames of antique garden benches into a stair railing, replacing their green paint with silver. Walls were coated with spray-on foam insulation followed by extra plaster so plates could be imbedded like tiles.

WHAT THE PROS KNOW ABOUT
TILE MOSAICS

Artist Hector Leonardi, designing this mosaic bath, avoided several common pitfalls: he used marble squares of identical thickness to avoid a bumpy surface; and except for thin ribbons of green tile around the tub, he did little cutting. He also confined complex tilework to small areas, like the "bathmat," an elaborate mosaic tabletop embedded in the floor. A simpler trompe l'oeil rug could be made with sheets of tiny colored tiles. Or, for economical custom work, hire a mosaic artist to do just a border, suggests Nancy A. Kintisch, owner of Off-White Castle Studio in Los Angeles. Work with a narrow palette to avoid visual chaos, she suggests. Cut as little tile as possible; sliced tile can be dangerously sharp. And plan patterns on graph paper, or, for an effect like Leonardi's, draw randomly from stacks of tiles organized by color.

Top left: Mann and Leonardi wrapped the walls and floor of the downstairs bath in a mosaic of marble tiles, all collected as samples and scraps from various marble yards. **Left and below:** Ceramic tile appears on the tub surround. French doors open the bath to the garden; an antique mosaic "rug" bears an appropriately aquatic theme.

Left: Mann replaced the old enamel on a vintage dental cabinet with lustrous silver leaf; the piece now holds towels in the bath. **Below:** A detail of mosaic on the wall above the tub. A ceramic tile border keeps the marble wall from appearing too cold and flat.

GENEROUSLY SCALED AND ARTFULLY BARE

Shaped like a shoebox, with pipes exposed and a ceiling so high as to seem aloof, a loft can be as challenging to furnish as an empty stage. But the owner of this 2,400-square-foot SoHo space, where rowboats and canoes were once manufactured, is a man who excels in set design. Alfredo Paredes, the vice president of creative services and Polo store development for Ralph Lauren, composes richly layered interiors for Lauren's stores worldwide. Accustomed to designing vignettes, Paredes parceled the 70-foot-long room into semiprivate zones without putting up full walls. "I didn't want to block the light," he says. "I still wanted the place to feel like a loft."

At the east end, where sun pours in through high, uncurtained windows, Paredes unfurled a sisal carpet and staged a living room within its borders: deep sofa and armchairs by Ralph Lauren, a coffee table on low, splaying legs by Christian Liagre. For the merest hint of enclosure, Paredes designed a standing glass screen, 10 feet tall and 10 feet wide, as a transparent curtain between the living and dining areas.

His palette, in shades of white and wheat, is more than neutral: it's ethereal. The walls, woodwork, and original beaded-board ceiling are painted in Benjamin Moore's Decorator White, with only honeyed wood and a few crisp lines of black for contrast. The result is an esthetic paradox, a space that looks half dressed but also complex, that feels airy yet simultaneously warm. To achieve it, Paredes chose fabrics and paint in creamy hues, and generously over-scaled his sparse furnishings. "The combination gives you both luxury and simplicity," he says. "It makes you feel invited."

Above: By propping artwork on the living-room floor and windowsill, Paredes created intimacy in oversized surroundings. Small objects read large when massed into compositions: white matte pottery, a mix of vintage Wedgwood and Bauer, gathers on a tabletop; a photograph of Paredes by David Seitner overlaps a 1930s drawing. **Left:** To keep his interior views free from clutter, Paredes built floor-to-ceiling closets, cabinetry, and picture ledges along a dining-area wall. The round table, a flea-market find, was stripped, bleached, and sealed; the skeletal iron chair, an English antique, was once used outdoors.

Left: Every piece in the living area contributes sculptural value—either curves, like the armchairs, or angles, like the art deco table with cascading ledges. **Below:** An immense leaning mirror brings reflected views to the desk. **Right:** Built-in shelves over the bed are three inches thick. (Skinny shelves, as Paredes puts it, look "nervous.")

WHAT THE PROS KNOW ABOUT
LEAVING WINDOWS BARE

By day, the artfully bare window—as opposed to the merely undressed—takes an architectural stand. "It feels big and empty and industrial," says Alfredo Paredes. In lieu of curtains, he leans a rotating gallery of pictures against the glass. By night, however, even a bare window with sweeping views will darken into a black hole. One solution: add discreet blinds or shades. New York designer Mariette Himes Gomez conceals them in a pocket that's recessed deep in the sill (for pull-up shades) or above the window (for roll-down blinds). "In the morning, the shade vanishes from sight," she says.

SUFFUSED WITH VIEWS: A FARMHOUSE RECONSIDERED

In rural Delaware County, New York, even the humblest 19th-century farmhouses play a classical note: Doric columns on the porch, perhaps, or a pediment over the door.

But the weekend home purchased by Rita Senders and Phil Silvestri, a New York couple with careers in advertising, made no attempt at grace. Built in 1939 to replace a farmhouse destroyed by fire, it was bereft of detail: no porch, no pillars, no connection between the interior and the surrounding 15 acres. Senders and Silvestri wanted to build it out, flush it with light, and give it a link to the past.

A 19th-century farm family would have added rooms in spurts as the children grew and had children of their own. Architect Marlys Hann simply sped up the process: she added four separate structures—portico, dining room, living room, and master bedroom—to the corners and sides of the existing home, as if its owners had prospered and spread out over generations. As a result, says Hann, "The house doesn't look new in the landscape. It just fits in."

The additions feel like pavilions, with so many tall windows and French doors that one would be hard-pressed to hang a painting. The little dining room is a dodecagon, with 10 of its 12 sides comprised largely of glass, and when the living room's seven pairs of French doors are all opened, entire walls melt away.

To accommodate all this glazing, Senders and Silvestri clustered their furnishings toward the center of the room, kindling intimacy in an expansive space. Both new rooms and old are faithful to the same details: Throughout, every wall is painted French vanilla (Benjamin Moore

Left: The dining room's conical ceiling peaks directly over the table, focusing attention on the company and the food. Nearly round, the 12-sided room is architect Marlys Hann's counterpoint to the square and rectangular additions. The custom-designed pedestal table is a play on the square porch columns. **Above:** To the back of the original house—the central, two-story section— Hann added a new living room, at right, and a master bedroom with its own narrow porch, at left. The base of each addition will be clad with local stone, in keeping with the neighboring farmhouses.

no. 190), every lighting fixture is in the Arts and Crafts style, and the Mission-style woodwork holds constant. "We decided at the beginning that the house would have harmony and continuity, so you're not moving from one design vignette to the next," says Senders.

Instead, fabrics and rough textures give these rooms their subtle distinction. The coffee table, an old, wide-board chest, still wears its original paint; the living-room rocker is made of bent twigs. "These are pieces our dads would use for firewood," says Senders. "But they really add a richness to the rooms."

Visitors, exploring, report a kind of exhilaration as they cross the threshold from the old house —which now holds the entry hall, library, and kitchen, with original nine-foot ceilings—into the gazebolike new rooms, where ceilings shaped like pyramids and cones ascend to nearly 17 feet. With that exalting contrast, "it feels like the space is expanding," says Hann. "I think you need that for your soul."

WHAT THE PROS KNOW ABOUT
FLOATING FURNITURE

When architect Marlys Hann designs a room, she invariably floats the furniture away from the walls. "It makes an intimate grouping in the center," she says, "and with oversized pieces, like Phil and Rita's sofa and lounge chair, you also get a feeling of spaciousness." She may fill in one side of the seating rectangle with a sofa and the others with four big lounge chairs; or she plants two sofas across from each other, with light, movable chairs at the other ends. Visitors, on entering, should see the front of the sofa, not the back, Hann advises. Finally, leave a path of at least 3½ feet between the sofa and the wall. The same principle works in other rooms. With three walls of windows in the bedroom, for example, Senders and Silvestri floated their tall bed, an iron four-poster, at an angle—aiming it straight toward a view of the pond.

Left: Because high ceilings are easily shrouded in shadow, Hann slipped indirect lighting behind the living room's flat crown moldings. The contemporary rug, designed by Timothy Van Campen, was the first purchase, and set the palette for upholstery fabrics. **Above.** Though not custom designed, the living room's French doors are eight feet tall, not the standard six-foot-eight. New flooring, used in every room, is rock maple, locally grown and milled.

Above: The graceful reproduction ironwork of twin beds is a guest room's major ornament. **Right:** A checkerboard floor in the guest bath was laid with vinyl to lower costs but turned on the diagonal to magnify space. Stairlike shelves were built to serve a reproduction claw-foot tub.

A COMFORTABLE HOME OF EXQUISITE RESTRAINT

With its deep-set porch, its dormers, and its turn-of-the-century graciousness, this Bridgehampton, Long Island, house shares a shingle-style vernacular with its neighbors. But there is less here than meets the eye, and deliberately so.

The porch columns are few, though they have sumo-wrestler stature. Those rear dormers have no mullions—each holds a single pane shaped like the archetypal Monopoly house. And inside, the easy esthetic is utterly without clichés: no slipcovers, no sisal, no summerhouse pastels. "Details in the house have a traditional basis, but they're done in a very stripped-to-the-basics way," says architect Peter Cook. "They're looked at as lines and shadows, not ornament. Everything has been taken to its simplest form."

Susan Sokol, a fashion-industry consultant, and her husband, Michael, who owns a textile company, wanted rooms whose bareness would create a sense of relief, not deprivation. Designer Mariette Himes Gomez thought in terms of letting the rooms breathe, with furnishings that merely hint at the ocean: "We planted subtle references to green in the McCoy pottery and celadon cushions," says Gomez. Because the house practically inhales its verdant lawns, thanks to long porches and interior corners enriched by windows, she could indulge in restraint. "The only real color is framed by the windows," says Gomez. "And there's so much to look at outside, these white rooms never feel empty."

To celebrate the living room's two-story height, Cook compressed the entry hall that leads into it, lowering its ceiling and elevating its floor. "You have a greater appreciation of a large room,"

Left: Columns appear in threes on each side of the house, their lines and heft adapted from the work of Victorian architect H. H. Richardson, who designed the first shingle-style house in 1874. Weathered floorboards imply the nearness of the ocean. **Top and above:** Front and back views of the house. Architect Peter Cook striped the gabled ends with cream-colored battens, a detail inspired by a shingled church nearby. He stained the shingles a dark tobacco color, not the typical sun-bleached gray of wooden beachfront homes: brown, he says, looks more honest for an inland house.

he explains, "if you enter it from a small one." Light pours down from the dormers, which serve here as skylights, and sifts through Gomez's unusual shutters—white fabric stretched taut between swiveling brass rods. They offer the softness of sheer material, but with a rigorous edge. "Some decorators keep adding to the picture; they keep piling it on, until you can't see the form underneath," says Gomez. "I tend to take things away." The result, she says, is a summerhouse ideal—"light and airy, and a place where the living is easy," she explains. "But also stylish, and pared down."

Opposite: Gomez was particularly conscious of texture in the living room. She upholstered the sofas with a piqué-like woven fabric and chose a rug woven in two shades of taupe. Walls are painted in Benjamin Moore's Brilliant White. **Top and left:** The dining room is a mix of mid-century modern—with chairs by Alvar Aalto—and the contemporary, with a table designed by Gomez. The windows wear her trademark fabric shutters. **Above:** Brightly colored prints were allowed to bloom only on the screened-in porch.

Far right: The kitchen's ease is expressed in its architecture, from a one-piece island that resembles two unrelated worktables to a varied skyline of cupboard heights. "Pieces farthest from the eating area are tall, while the cabinetry nearest the table is lower and smaller, encouraging informality," notes the kitchen designer, Joan Picone. **Right:** A built-in hutch appears freestanding, like farmhouse furniture. Like the refrigerator, it is sheathed in beadboard. **Below:** The island's pillarlike supports are Picone's tribute to the bulging porch columns outside.

WHAT THE PROS KNOW ABOUT
COLLECTING ART POTTERY

A purist can pay $3,000 at auction for a Newcomb College vase. But $25 to $75 at a flea market can still buy well-designed art pottery, like the graceful McCoy vases and pitchers that designer Mariette Himes Gomez assembled in this Long Island house. Pieces in this price range are not turn-of-the-century Arts and Crafts pieces, but factory-made versions—often produced for florists—from the 1940s and 1950s. Names like Shawnee, Red Wing, Weller, and Cowan may appear on the base of florist ware; just as often, there's no mark at all, says Terry Kovel, co-author of *Kovels' Antiques & Collectibles Price List.* And Niloak pottery, expensive when marbleized, sells for a song when plain. Massed together for impact, postwar art pottery has strong decorative value. Buy for love, advises the Boston design firm C & J Katz, but collect with a focus. Settle on one or two colors, and on matte or shiny glaze. Vary the sizes—partly to give the grouping an arresting skyline, and partly to have a wide range of vases on hand for use.

Above and right: The master bedroom is uncorked at the top by a windowed tower, 18 feet high and full of sky. Beneath it, walls begin their atticlike slope only six feet from the floor, establishing a more human scale. To make the bedroom seem dreamy almost to the point of weightlessness, Gomez floated sheer curtains in the windows, then painted walls, woodwork, and ceiling with a single hue, Benjamin Moore's Super White. To anchor the room, she wove through it a few mahogany furnishings that register as ebony. **Left:** For the master bath, a mosaic floor of tumbled marble was chosen for its shell-colored pallor.

NEW
ENGLAND

FROM COUNTRY FARMHOUSE TO URBAN
BOATHOUSE, THESE HOMES ARE
SPARKED WITH A FEELING OF LIFE, FAMILY,
AND STYLISH DOMESTICITY

225

On an avenue in Cambridge near Harvard Square stands a row of old, patrician homes. Behind them, tucked judiciously away on a cul-de-sac, are the half-dozen "worker's cottages" that once served them—diminutive houses, built solidly but without pretense in the 1920s, that make up in charm what they lack in grandeur.

Several cottages have since been enlarged, but this one, with just three rooms downstairs, was expanded in spirit only. Its designers, Cheryl and Jeffrey Katz of the Boston firm C & J Katz, painted its rooms in shades of green and blue that might have sifted in like mist. As a result, a visitor experiences the walls of these little rooms not as boundaries, but as cool, atmospheric color. And since the rooms are arranged *en enfilade*—all visible from the foyer, and each pouring into the next—the gentle chromatic shifts underscore the flow, not the division, of space.

"The house is very sweet, and it would be easy to do a lot of florals," says Cheryl Katz, "but we were inspired by simple Swedish interiors from the 1800s. We used colors that were grayed down, which is like adding a few drops of black to a clear, strong color. A grayed or 'dirty' color is more subtle, yet it doesn't wash out in the sunlight."

The small foyer is painted a yellow-tinged color that the Katzes fondly call "icky green" (Benjamin

Right: The dining room, despite the grid of the checked slipcovers on its chairs, is largely defined by curves— from the meandering vines of a 1930s Chinese art deco rug to the doors of an anigre-veneer cabinet designed by Jeffrey Katz.

Moore's HC-1, a historic color). To its right is the sage-green living room (HC-114); to its left, the steel-blue dining room (HC-146). Throughout the house, moldings and woodwork are painted a warm, full-spectrum white (Benjamin Moore's White Dove) that gives the muddied hues a pristine clarity.

In rooms where Victorian rugs might be expected, the Katzes unfurled a Tibetan carpet and a restrained Chinese art deco rug. The curtains, too, might have been borrowed from an urban apartment; they are veils of sheer linen, without fuss or finials. Where passing references to cottage style do appear, they are largely confined to fabrics, and kept unusually spare: bright yellow checks are overscaled, which gives them a graphic sophistication, and a companion stripe appears not on the expected printed cotton, but on a substantial woven material.

Opposite: The Katzes found an antique Scandinavian table for the dining room and had a leaf made to expand it. The antique Swedish sofa serves as a banquette; though it set the tone for the house, its upright stance was more suited to dining than to living-room lounging. **Left:** To focus attention on the sofa's curvaceous form, upholstery was confined to a solid color with only the slight accent of yellow-striped welting. **Below:** The foyer, minimally furnished with an umbrella stand, empties into the living room just beyond. As in every room, generous white woodwork acts as a frame for planes of color.

The cottage's reigning piece of furniture, a 19th-century Swedish sofa with an undulating wood frame, holds court in the dining room. As the first major purchase for the house, it dented an already limited budget—but it also launched the theme of Scandinavian simplicity that came to govern these rooms. Jeffrey, in homage to the sofa's curves, designed an accompanying cabinet with a wavelike facade.

"In every project there has to be one thing you completely fall in love with, even if it's expensive," says Cheryl. "For our client, it was this sofa. We bought chairs from Crate & Barrel, and we used pricey fabrics mostly in small touches, like pillows. But finding this sofa was a defining moment, and it made the house sing."

Left: In the living room, the overmantel area was left bare, a triumph of color over ornament. A persimmon chair and Tibetan rug add a snap of color to an otherwise serene space.

WHAT THE PROS KNOW ABOUT
SHEER CURTAINS

A sheer gives shape to the unseen breeze, filters the glare out of sunlight, admits a hint of the view, and offers a measure of privacy, not to mention romance. These, by designers Cheryl and Jeffrey Katz, are a loose-weave linen—but could just as easily be lightweight wool, cotton, silk, or polyester (often marketed under its French name, *tergal*). For a modern, architectural look, advises Jeffrey Katz, use ungathered panels that hang flat, like banners; for lush, traditional drapery, make your sheers $2\frac{1}{2}$ to 3 times as wide as the curtain rod. The Katzes' top four tips:

- Make the drapery long enough to touch the floor without puddling.

- Install pull-down shades or wood blinds behind the fabric—not just for privacy, but to delay the inevitable: any unlined fabric exposed to sun will eventually fade or rot. (You'll get longer life from polyester, cotton, and wool than from linen and silk; budget accordingly.)

- Unweighted sheers can billow into a room like sails; to ground them somewhat, have a beaded chain stitched into the hem.

- Fold the top edge over the front of the drapery, creating an apron 6 to 12 inches long; the higher the ceiling, advise the Katzes, the longer the apron.

Big house, little house, back house, barn. This snippet of a child's rhyme drifted back to Claudia Sargent as she described to her architects the weekend house she wanted: not a replica of an antiquated farmhouse, but a modern home that would appear to have stood on its site for generations.

The rhyme said it perfectly: a New England telescoping house in which the main structure, or big house, was enlarged over time by annexes, like graduated pearls. And like any self-respecting Vermont farmhouse, this one, designed by Debra Wassman and Jonathan Lanman of Trumbull Architects in New York, is embraced by a wraparound front porch. Its high transom windows are reminiscent of those in the region's sugaring shacks, where sap is heated and steam must find an exit.

Yet no one would mistake this house for something old—not with a "barn" that proves to be a garage; not with a kitchen ceiling that rises, in a generous and contemporary gesture, more than 10 feet high; and not with proportions that follow the laws of geometry instead of history. "We isolated the architectural elements of an old house," explains Wassman, and they reinterpreted them in a truly contemporary fashion.

Sargent, a psychotherapist, and her husband, Paul Feinberg, a lawyer, presented Wassman with a wish list drawn partly from Sargent's childhood. She wanted rooms that felt gracefully half bare, with tall, undressed windows, because they reminded her of a Victorian house where she had played as a girl. And she wanted a kitchen that no one could bear to leave:

Above: Seen from behind, the house proceeds from a formal living room at left (with a small study bumped out at its far end) to the central kitchen (where four windows, strung together, create a bay for the dining table). Between them is a short connecting link, or hyphen. At far right is a mudroom.

WHAT THE PROS KNOW ABOUT
SHAKER STYLE

It took more than pared-down proportions and pumpkin-colored stain to give Claudia Sargent's kitchen its warm yet minimalist Shaker esthetic. She also had to give up anything that looked bulky or busy, from upper cabinets and spice racks to displays of her Italian faience pottery. For storage, architect Debra Wassman adapted a wall of built-in floor-to-ceiling cabinetry from pictures and surviving Shaker examples. Drawer depths are graduated (deepest on the bottom, shallowest on top), and Benjamin Moore's Honey Maple stain provides the traditional amber glow. For inspiration, Sargent and Wassman pored over *Shaker: Life, Work, and Art*, by June Sprigg and David Larkin, and sketched cabinetry at the Shaker Museum and Library in Old Chatham, New York (518.794.9100). Books of carpentry plans can be ordered through the museum's Web site (www.shakermuseumoldchat.org) and sympathetic furnishings are sold by Shaker Workshops (catalog, 781.646.8985). Restraint, however, comes only from within, as Wassman knew when she chose not to panel the black General Electric refrigerator. "I think people are wary of something that has a Shaker facade," she explains, "and a through-the-door ice maker."

reparation for all the childhood nights when her mother had announced, "Let's retire to the living room," stanching the most spirited conversations.

Not surprisingly, Sargent rejected a formal dining room. Instead, a windowed niche off the kitchen is furnished with a banquette and 10-foot-long table. Closer to the cook, a floor-to-ceiling bank of Shaker-style drawers and cupboards offers storage, as do pegs, cubbies, and shelves—everything but overhead cabinets. They were banned, Wassman explains, to make the kitchen look more like a family room.

Sargent's decorating strategy was to give the rooms air. The lamps are black silhouettes; window shades are white linen, with schoolhouse pulls. No hanging pictures affront the walls. Friendly proportions, lacking ornament, make each room intimate. "There's nothing gratuitous in sight," says Wassman, "and that lets the house stand on its own."

Left: In the kitchen's dining niche, Wassman aligned the top of the custom-made table (crafted from antique floorboards) with the windowsills. **Above:** In the master bedroom's house-shaped sleeping nook, the headboard is terraced for extra storage. **Above right.** Architect Debra Wassman adapted classic Shaker designs for a kitchen wall of floor-to-ceiling storage.

THROWING A CURVE AT A CLASSICAL HOUSE

Lydia Shire's house greets the street with a temperate Greek Revival facade, respectful of its neighbors and its own late-18th-century past. But if the front of this 10-room house plays like classical music, the interior is as vibrant as jazz.

Gold leaf glimmers on the dining-room ceiling. Walls are sometimes sinuous instead of straight. A living-room column, broad-shouldered at the top, tapers to a cuff of molding like an architectural zoot suit. And the back of the house is a two-story curving wall of glass.

For all its apparent improvisation, the redesign adheres to principles nearly as rigorous as those governing the neoclassical shell. "I set up some rules from the beginning," says architect Lisa Shire, who handled the renovation for her mother. "Everything that was original to the house stayed orthogonal—perpendicular, or 90 degrees. Everything new could curve, or be different. I never tried to make new elements look old."

Lydia Shire, who owns the Boston restaurants Biba and Pignoli, has tastes that were deeply

Right: The house had been abandoned for five years, with squirrels living indoors and rain dripping through the roof. **Far right:** After decorative painter Iris Lee Marcus put down her graining tools, the yellow living-room walls looked like silk moiré. Lydia Shire designed her own velvet sofa, and she upholstered floor pillows in kilim rugs. Bill Thompson, an artist friend, painted *Wall Eyes* (at right) after commenting that the room lacked only a water view.

Left: Architect Lisa Shire gave her mother a glass-walled pantry, with a floor-to-ceiling window that mimics the dimensions of the doorway. Open shelves focus attention on Lydia's copper cookware. **Right:** The kitchen was designed around a red Chambers stove from the 1930s or 1940s, purchased by Lydia years before she actually had a place for it. To give the ceiling a hue like that of the concrete floor, painter Iris Lee Marcus stirred a dollop of white into Benjamin Moore's HC 124.

influenced by her own parents, both artists. She wanted passionate, high-gloss color to pulse on the walls. She wanted ebonized wood floors that would shine like obsidian. And she wanted asymmetry in the overall design, as befits a woman whose plates, chairs, even drawer knobs refuse to match. "My parents told me, when they were painting or drawing in their studio, that nothing in life is ever symmetrical," says Lydia. "That's always stayed with me."

Even as the pillared front of the house was being restored, Lisa was slicing off the back. The kitchen (downstairs) and master bedroom (directly above it) were rebuilt and sheathed with a wall of huge glass panes in a red metal framework. The glass wall curves, which makes the boundary between the rooms and the fields seem evanescent. "I sometimes walk into the kitchen and think that the counter has leaves on it," says Lydia. The polished concrete floor looks like stone; the ceiling, painted a similar color, gleams in sunlight.

Confronting a major interior wall that bisects the house, Lisa took the longest distance between two points and nudged it into a languid curve. In the dining room, where the undulating plaster faces leaf-green walls, decorative artist Iris Lee Marcus applied a frescolike finish in marigold hues. "On every floor, you experience the curved wall in different ways, and see it in different colors," says Lisa Shire. "But it's a unifying theme. By staying with one strong concept, I was able to keep the house surprisingly simple."

WHAT THE PROS KNOW ABOUT
EBONIZED FLOORS

Contrary to its name, an ebonized floor is not always pure black. Though true ebony stains exist, Lydia Shire's floors are a rich brown-black—a color customized for her by John Brady, then with contractor CAFCO Development. Pure black, notes Brady, tends to obscure the wood grain. His recipe: after the final sanding and a thorough vacuuming, mop the floor with plain cold water to raise the grain, making it more receptive to stain. Let it dry to the touch. Apply a mix of 50 percent dark walnut stain and 50 percent red mahogany (both Minwax colors). Let dry. Apply a second coat. When thoroughly dry, do a light sanding, also called a screening. Seal with several coats of oil-based polyurethane. Shire used high-gloss; it shows scratches more easily than a satin finish, but gave her the shine she desired. *Tip:* Sanding machines can seriously gouge a floor; unless you have done the job before, hire a professional.

Opposite: The dining-room fireplace, once white brick, was rebuilt in lacewood with North African tile. A full spectrum of gold—in the gilded ceiling, gold mesh swag, and honey-colored sisal—warms the room. Stem-colored walls are painted with Benjamin Moore no. 635. **Above left:** The kitchen's modern glass wall is surrounded by materials with a sense of the past, from New England fieldstone to barn-red siding. The glass panes narrow from one end of the bowed window to the other, accentuating the curve. **Left:** The master bedroom, with its glass wall, appears to float over the fields. A 19th-century cockfighting chair was designed to be straddled; its writing ledge allowed a user to record bets while watching the fights.

Most mornings at 6 A.M., George Germon and Johanne Killeen, married owners of the
Providence restaurant Al Forno, are awakened by the sound of drilling. "I love it," says
Germon. "We live in a working boatyard, and we love the atmosphere." The boatyard lies
along Narragansett Bay, where Germon and Killeen's 60-foot boathouse floated on a barge
until it was permanently moored in the 1920s on solid ground.

"It was really basic when we bought it," says Germon. "You could see the bones of the roof,
the windows were single-glazed, and the space was one big room." Now it looks more like a
floating château, thanks to water views from nearly every window and a sense of formality that
was carried through the renovation. Germon, who taught at the Rhode Island School of
Design before opening Al Forno, and Killeen, a former freelance photographer, found numerous ways to suggest old-world glamour. They built a small vestibule at the top of the entry
stairs, and enclosed it with salvaged glass-paned doors (replacing some clear panes with
antique lilac glass). With lengths of molding, they gave their plain walls a dressy *rinceau* treatment, painting some of the smaller panels to resemble gold and silver leaf. They set the
bedroom apart with old, stripped French doors that wear the patina of age. And they striped
the living-room ceiling in sophisticated sky colors of celadon and lavender, adding a layer of
pattern overhead while keeping the furnishings spare.

Living-room floorboards were battleship gray under the previous owner's reign; now they are
painted the palest green. An overlay of antique Oriental rugs, arrayed like stepping-stones,

Left: Even the smallest architectural details convey elegance—like the tiny inset squares of mirror installed above the pilasters around the vestibule. After Germon painted stripes on the ceiling, he sealed his work with blue chalk lines intact: "It strengthens the edge of each color," he says. **Above:** Behind a 19th-century table in the living room, squares of mirror (above) and salvaged Victorian tiles (below) are embedded in a wall panel painted moss green.

leads visitors from the vestibule at one end to a new eat-in kitchen (replacing an old Pullman unit) at the other. Germon and Killeen designed the kitchen in stainless steel, and by banishing overhead cupboards, they created a workspace as clean-lined as a laboratory. But when Germon sheathed the walls with an unexpected veneer of Connecticut bluestone, he indulged a lifelong yearning: "I've always wanted a stone house," he admits. With the marriage of cool steel to craggy bluestone, he proves that a kitchen of restaurant-caliber efficiency can still be a balm for the soul.

Left: Substantial crown moldings, installed by Germon and Killeen, visually heighten the living-room ceiling and give the space architectural stature. French doors, at right, partition off the bedroom without blocking light. At the far end, a rarely used freight door was ornamented with gold paint. **Above:** Using simple stock molding, Germon framed out square and rectangular panels on every wall; within their borders, he staged symmetrical, carefully edited vignettes.

Above: The stainless-steel kitchen is made humane by
tactile materials, including a pine ceiling and mirrored
squares embedded like jewels above the range. The
kitchen chairs once belonged to Killeen's parents. **Right:**
Inspired by the floors of the Basilica di San Marco in
Venice, Germon pieced together his own mosaic floor for
the downstairs entry using marble and other stone tiles,
mostly samples from suppliers and stores. **Opposite:**
Stairs lead from the front door up to the vestibule. A
glass-block window on the left is balanced, on the right,
by framed wood panels that grow progressively narrower
as one ascends.

WHAT THE PROS KNOW ABOUT
TOUCHES OF GOLD

Louis XIV knew the value of decorating with gold: it emanated luxury, reflected light, ennobled everything it touched—hence Versailles. For his boathouse, however, George Germon applied gold with a casual twist: he paneled the walls with molding, then "gilded" the smaller insets with gold and silver acrylic paint. (His recipe: Apply a base coat of silver paint, thinned to the consistency of light cream. When dry, mask off small squares that are slightly out of kilter; fill in with thinned gold paint.) New York interior designer Marshall Watson, who holds that no room is finished without glimpses of gold, offers a few more ways to work it in:

- Use lampshades in lacquered green, maroon, or black, with gold paper lining.

- Collect old gilded frames to use with mirrors or art.

- Replace old hinges and doorknobs with brass fittings.

- Stencil a dark wood floor with an understated pattern in gold leaf.

- Use gold-colored rings and finials when hanging curtains. But make the rods wood, not brass: "You don't want to get too Louis unless you're Louis," Watson cautions, then paraphrases Chanel: "When you think you have enough gold in the room, step back and remove one thing."

Left: Stock crown molding, affixed to the ceiling over the bed, offers the essence of a canopy without the fuss of fabric. Panels on either side of the French doors are textured opaque glass; the icons that lie against them are suspended from fine wire.

RESOURCES

ARCHITECTS AND DESIGNERS: A listing of the design professionals featured in the book.

The information that follows is provided as a service. It was current at the time of publication.

Michael Anderson
Clacton & Frinton
107 South Robertson Blvd.
Los Angeles, California 90048
310.275.1967; 213.653.2286

Robert D. Ascione, Architect
Design Collective of New York
114 West 17th Street
New York, New York 10011
212.255.2255

Edward Asfour and Peter Guzy
Asfour Guzy Architects
594 Broadway, Suite 1204
New York, New York 10012
212.334.9350

Patrick Bell and David Guilmet
Bell-Guilmet Associates
6465 Route 202
New Hope, Pennsylvania 18938
215.862.2490

Charles Bohl and Barbara Bohl
Bohl Architects
161 Prince George Street
Annapolis, Maryland 21401
410.263.2200

Laura Bohn
L.B.D.A.
30 West 26th Street, 11th floor
New York, New York 10010
212.645.3636

**Thomas L. Bosworth FAIA
Architect**
4532 East Laurel Drive Northeast
Seattle, Washington 98105
206.522.5549

Stephen Brady
29 East Ninth Street, Suite 12A
New York, New York 10003
212.982.7077

Peter F. Carlson, L.L.C.
162 Joshuatown Road
Lyme, Connecticut 06371
860.434.3744

Linda Chase Associates
482 Town Street
East Haddam, Connecticut 06423
860.873.9499

Annie Chu
Chu + Gooding Architects
2020 North Main Street
Los Angeles, California 90031
213.222.6268

Peter Cook Architect
280 Elm Street
Southampton, New York 11963
516.283.0077

Carl D'Aquino
Carl D'Aquino Interiors
180 Varick Street
New York, New York 10014
212.929.9787

John Marsh Davis
96 Santa Rosa
Sausalito, California 94965

Duany Plater-Zyberk
1023 S.W. 25th Avenue
Miami, Florida 33135
305.644.1023

Michael Graves Architect
341 Nassau Street
Princeton, New Jersey 08540
609.924.6409

Gwynn Griffith Design
214 Regent
San Antonio, Texas 78204
210.533.6465

Marlys Hann Architect
52 West 84th Street
New York, New York 10024
212.787.1680

**James Hanson and Stephen
Douthit**
American Island Home and Garden
Design
3505 West 44th Street
Minneapolis, Minnesota 55410
612.925.9006

Mariette Himes Gomez
Gomez Associates
504-506 East 74th Street
New York, New York 10021
212.288.6856

Holden & Dupuy
3420 Magazine Street, Suite C
New Orleans, Louisiana 70115
504.897.1100

Israel Callas Shortridge Associates
254 South Robertson Boulevard,
Suite 205
Beverly Hills, California 90211
310.652.8087

C & J Katz Studio
60 K Street
South Boston, Massachusetts
02127
617.464.0330

Lake/Flato Architects
311 Third Street, Suite 200
San Antonio, Texas 78205
210.227.3335

Paul Lamb Architects
618 Lavaca Street, Room 9
Austin, Texas 78701
512.478.7316

Mell Lawrence Architects
913 Gibson Street
Austin, Texas 78704
512.441.4669

Joseph Lembo
Joseph Lembo Industries
666 Greenwich Street, Suite 739
New York, New York 10014
212.463.7871

also: **Joseph Lembo Industries
at C.I.A., Inc.**
6-15 Udagawa cho,
Shibuya-ku
Tokyo 150 Japan
011-81-3-3464-5690

Barbara Lione
Interiors II
1827 North Sedgwick
Chicago, Illinois 60614
312.280.8260

Thomas McCallum, A.I.A.
1932 First Avenue, Suite 703
Seattle, Washington 98101
206.441.1596

Roy McMakin
1422 34th Avenue
Seattle, Washington 98122
206.323.0111

also: Roy McMakin
6150 Wilshire Boulevard,
Space 6
Los Angeles, California
90036
213.936.8206

Lisa B. Shire
533 East 83rd Street, Suite 1C
New York, New York 10028
212.472.0051
lisabshire@juno.com

Michael S. Smith
1454 Fifth Street
Santa Monica, California 90401
310.656.5733

Susan Schuyler Smith
Spectrum
6000 North A1A
Vero Beach, Florida 32963

Trelles Architects
169 East Flagler Street, Suite 828
Miami, Florida 33131
305.373.1960

Patrick Wade
31 North Moore Street, Penthouse
New York, New York 10013
212.226.4904

Debra Wassman and Jonathan Lanman
Trumbull Architects
225 Lafayette Street
New York, New York 10012
212.226.5331

REGIONAL RESOURCES: A regional listing of stores featured in the book. The information that follows is provided as a service. It was current at the time of publication.

CALIFORNIA
BERKELEY

The Gardener
1836 Fourth Street
Berkeley, California 94710
510.548.4545
The store that started garden style.

Zia
1310 Tenth Street
Berkeley, California 94710
510.528.2337
Unusual, appealing mix of furniture
and accessories from around the
country.

BEVERLY HILLS

Livingstones
345 North Canon Drive
Beverly Hills, California 90210
310.278.7970
Luxury and custom linens for table,
bath, and bed.

Room with a View
1600 Montana Avenue
Santa Monica, California 90403
310.998.5858
Furnishings, linens, and accessories
for bed, bath, and kitchen. "A little of
everything, done tastefully," writes
city editor Laura Hull.

LOS ANGELES

Anichini
466 North Robertson Boulevard
Los Angeles, California 90048
310.657.4292
Linens of exquisite luxury, silk-bound
cashmere blankets; linen sheets.

Baldacchino
919 La Cienega Street
Los Angeles, California 90069
310.657.6810
Asian and European antiques with a
great sense of delicacy; 18th-century
French pieces are a specialty.

Blackman Cruz
800 North La Cienega Boulevard
Los Angeles, California 90069
313.657.9228
Idiosyncratic, 20th-century, one-of-a-
kind furniture, lighting, and art.

Blueprint
8366 Beverly Boulevard
Los Angeles, California 90048
213.653.2439
A 15,000-square-foot emporium of
Italian furnishings for home and
office: desks, beds, wall units, lighting, dining tables, and more.

Demolicious
7912 Melrose Avenue
Los Angeles, California 90046
213.655.6600
Salvaged, antique, and architectural
home furnishings, from late-19th-
century steel furniture and cast-iron
benches to columns, finials, and
corbels.

Diamond Foam & Fabric
611 South La Brea Avenue
Los Angeles, California 90036
213.931.8148
A famous source for well-priced
fabrics.

Diva
8801 Beverly Boulevard
Los Angeles, California 94008
310.278.3191
The best contemporary European,
mainly Italian, design and lighting.

Domestic Furniture
6150 Wilshire Boulevard, Space 6
Los Angeles, California 90036
213.936.8206
Roy McMakin's wood and upholstered
furniture. Also custom furnishings.

Duson Design Entity
7918 Melrose Avenue
Los Angeles, California 90046
213.651.0521
Formerly Son Collections, this store
sells Asian antiques, American folk
art, and small furnishings on the
scale of tables and chairs.

Linea
8843-49 Beverly Boulevard
Los Angeles, California 90016
310.273.5425
The Los Angeles branch of Ligne
Roset, offering the newest in
European design.

Liz's Antique Hardware
453 South La Brea Avenue
Los Angeles, California 90036
800.939.9003
Hardware for windows, doors, and
more. Some dates to 1850, but Liz
also stocks reproductions and new,
artistic pieces.

Modernica
7366 Beverly Boulevard
Los Angeles, California 90036
213.933.0383
Modernist furniture from the 1920s
to the 1960s, plus reproductions of
the classics. Also in Chicago and
New York.

Modern Living
4063 Redwood Avenue
Los Angeles, California 90066
213.655.3898
One of the top purveyors of contemporary furniture, both European and
American, as well as classic reissues.

Paul Ferrante
8464 Melrose Place
Los Angeles, California 90069
213.653.4142
Antique armoires, console tables,
and other antiques, mostly 18th- and
19th-century French and English
pieces. "A small, personal shop,
loaded to the ceiling," writes city
editor Laura Hull.

Plug
8017 Melrose Avenue
Los Angeles, California 90046
323.653.5635
A great selection of innovative
European lighting.

Rubbish
1630 Silverlake Boulevard
Los Angeles, California 90026
213.661.5575
Furniture, lighting, and accessories
from the 1940s through the 1970s,
including Knoll, Herman Miller, and
some Danish pieces; also Asian furnishings. "Owner Scott Mangan has
a great eye for treasures," writes
Laura Hull.

Silk Trading Company
360 La Brea Avenue
Los Angeles, California 90036
213.954.9280
Opulent yet affordable fabrics.

Virtue
149 South La Brea Avenue
Los Angeles, California 90069
213.932.1789
Rustic and distressed furniture and
accessories.

SAN FRANCISCO

Clervi Marble
221 Bayshore Boulevard
San Francisco, California 94124
415.648.7165
"Eighty-year-old source for noble and
beautiful natural stones," writes *Met
Home* city editor Diane Dorrans
Saeks. Countertops and tabletops
made.

deVera
580 Sutter Street
San Francisco, California 94192
415.989.0988
Small specialty store that offers
antiques as well as pieces designed
by the owner.

Earthsake
2076 Chestnut Street
San Francisco, California 94123
415.441.2896
Ecologically friendly tableware, furniture, linens, and accessories. (Also in
Berkeley and Palo Alto.)

Ed Hardy San Francisco
188 Henry Adams Street
San Francisco, California 94103
415.626.6300
Antiques of all provenances:
Venetian, Moroccan, Continental,
Asian, English, and American; also
"elegant, witty painted furniture,"
notes Saeks.

Fillamento
2185 Fillmore Street
San Francisco, California 94115
415.931.2224
An important store with three floors
of furniture, tableware, and glass,
with works by local talent like Ann
Gish and Annieglass.

Gumps
135 Post Street
San Francisco, California 94108
415.982.1616
The biggest selection of tableware,
plus Asian articles and crafts.

Ligne & Co.
760 Market Street
San Francisco, California 94102
415.956.7125
Furniture, accessories, and lighting
by Andree Putman, Philippe Starck,
Mathiew & Ray for Ecart, and top
California talent such as Sandback
Design, Alan Sklansky, and Greg
Benke.

Mike Furniture
2142 Fillmore Street
San Francisco, California 94115
415.767.2700
Classic, comfortable upholstery,
tables, and cabinets.

**San Francisco MoMA Museum
Shop**
151 Third Street
San Francisco, California 94108
415.357.4035
Selection represents the work of tal-
ented young designers.

Sue Fisher King
3067 Sacramento Street
San Francisco, California 94115
415.922.7276
A stylish mix of European and
American tableware, candles, and
soap.

Zinc Details
1905 Fillmore Street
San Francisco, California 94115
415.776.2100
Furniture, lighting, and accessories
with a modern aesthetic; most
designed in-house.

SANTA MONICA

Dormire
1345 Fourth Street
Santa Monica, California 90401
310.393.9288 or 888-DORMIRE
A sleek, warm shop that stocks
Italian imports for the bedroom: bed-
frames, Flou beds, duvets, pillows,
Dormire linens, bedside tables; also
bath accessories.

High Light
2427 Main Street
Santa Monica, California 90405
310.450.5886
Designer Ron Rezek offers a well-
edited range of contemporary
lighting.

Jasper
1454 Fifth Street
Santa Monica, California 90401
310.656.5733
The 7,000-square-foot atelier of interior designer Michael Smith, stocked
with antique furniture and accessories, linens, art, glass, Donald
Kaufman paints, and Smith's own
designs.

JohnSaintDenis
1408 Montana Avenue
Santa Monica, California 90403
310.393.1801 or 800.217.9500
Antiques, custom furnishings, and an
in-house design library for
inspiration.

VENICE

Ilan Dei
1227 Abbot Kinney
Venice, California 90291
310.450.0999
Modern objects for the home—candlesticks, mirrors, sofas, chairs,
clocks—mostly of aluminum, maple,
and cherry, designed by owner Ilan
Dei in a style he calls "lush
minimalism."

Modernaires
1237 Abbot Kinney Boulevard
Venice, California 90291
310.452.4119
High-style furnishings by 20th-
century California modernist designers, including Paul Frankl, Paul
Laszlo, Van Keppel-Green, and
Gilbert Rohde.

WEST HOLLYWOOD

Details
8625½ Melrose Avenue
West Hollywood, California 90069
310.659.1550
House fittings of all kinds: mail-
boxes, granite sinks, hardware for the
bath, and a mix of country French
and contemporary furnishings.

James Jennings
8471 Melrose Avenue
West Hollywood, California 90069
213.655.7823
Finely crafted furniture by top interior
designers as well as Jennings's own
line.

Statewide

Golden Goose
45094 Main Street
Mendocino, California 95460
707.937.4655
Fine European linens, Egyptian cotton towels, French soaps, and items
for the bar.

Gordon Bennett
1129 Howard Avenue
Burlingame, California 94010
650.401.3647
Home and garden furnishings: topiaries, fountains, outdoor sculpture,
hand-blown glass.

Luciano Antiques
San Carlos Street and Fifth Avenue
Carmel, California 93921
408.624.9396
A trove of antique and reproduction
furniture, with an emphasis on 17th-
and 18th-century Mediterranean
styles, also lighting, sculpture, and
accessories.

Millstreet
1131 Chestnut Street
Menlo Park, California 94025
650.323.9010
Bed linens by Ann Gish, pottery from
Tuscany, mirrors, botanical prints,
and antiques.

Modern I
500 Red Hill Avenue
San Anselmo, California 94960
415.456.3960
Mid-century furnishings, including
Eames chairs and furniture designed
by architects.

The Phoenix
Highway 1
Big Sur, California 93920
408.667.2347
Imported decorative objects and furnishings: teak benches, ceramics,
glass, stepping stones, fountains.

Rose Bowl Flea Market
1001 Rose Bowl Drive
Pasadena, California 91103
213.588.4411
Vintage furniture, Hollywood memo-
rabilia; a major market with 2,200
vendors, held the second Sunday of
every month.

SummerHouse Gallery
21 Throckmorton Street
Mill Valley, California 94941
415.383.6695
Frames, glassware, candlesticks,
slipcovered loveseats, and other necessary luxuries. "Impossible to leave
empty-handed," writes Diane
Dorrans Saeks.

MID-ATLANTIC
DELAWARE

Affordable Antique Mall
4300 Highway 1
Rehobeth Beach, Delaware 19971
302.227.5803
A cluster of 25 dealers, open daily
April through October, closed
Wednesdays other months.
Furniture, glassware, china, and
books, from early 19th century
through the 1960s.

Bellefonte Resale Shop
901 Brandywine Boulevard
Wilmington, Delaware 19809
302.762.1885
A changing assortment of antique to
contemporary furniture and collectibles of every vintage.

The Garage Sale
1416 Route 1
Lewes, Delaware 19958
302.645.1205
Five buildings packed with architectural and garden pieces, iron gates, statuary, good antique furnishings, and lots
of 1950s furniture. A favorite among
Washington, D.C., interior designers.

NEW JERSEY

Cassidy & Co.
2 Lincoln Place
Madison, New Jersey 07940
973.593.6826
Hand-painted furnishings and accessories, including armoires, tables,
chairs, and lamps.

**Christopher Brandner Design
Solutions**
51 Silverbrook Road
Shrewsbury, New Jersey 07702
732.224.8692
Open largely by appointment.
Lusciously upholstered furniture:
watch for chairs with leopard-print
seats and swirly metal arms and legs.
Also custom furnishings in wrought
iron, cast metal, upholstery, glass,
and wood.

Englishtown Auction Sales
90 Wilson Avenue
Englishtown, New Jersey 07751
732.446.9644
Saturdays and Sundays year-round.
Established in 1929, this 100-acre
open-air market bills itself as
"affordable."

Graves Design Collection
338 Nassau Street
Princeton, New Jersey 08540
609.497.6878
Elegant and witty objects designed by
architect Michael Graves: candlesticks, lighting fixtures, clocks, book-
ends, frames and, of course, that
famous teapot.

Lambertville Antique Market
1864 River Road
Lambertville, New Jersey 08530
609.397.0456
Antiques and collectibles sold
Saturdays and Sundays year-round;
additional indoor shops open on
Wednesdays.

O'valé
2 Broad Street
Red Bank, New Jersey 07701
908.933.0437
Modern furniture, lighting, and
accessories—a vast selection of
classics by Eames, Noguchi, Knoll,
Herman Miller, and Thonet; also new
pieces from Cassina, Flos, Kartell,
and Alessi.

PENNSYLVANIA

Anthropologie
201 West Lancaster Avenue
Wayne, Pennsylvania 19087
610.687.4141
Found objects and reproductions, all
with a measure of patina or rust: furniture, mirrors, candlesticks, drawer
pulls, frames, and more. Also in
Maryland, Connecticut, New York,
California, and Illinois.

Architectural Antiques Exchange
715 North Second Street
Philadelphia, Pennsylvania 19123
215.922.3669
Architectural salvage: doors, mantels,
paneling, sinks, and Victorian built-in
wardrobes, rescued from late-19th-
century Philadelphia houses.

Iron Apple Forge
Routes 263 and 413
(mailing address: P.O. Box 724)
Buckingham, Pennsylvania 18912
215.794.7351
Wrought-iron and hand-crafted lighting fixtures for indoors and out;
chandeliers, pot racks, and garden
accessories.

Material Culture
4700 Wissahickon Avenue
Philadelphia, Pennsylvania 19144
215.849.8030
A 25,000-square-foot emporium of
rustic furnishings and wares from
Turkey, India, the Balkans, and
China.

Moderne Gallery
111 North Third Street
Philadelphia, Pennsylvania 19106
215.923.8536
French and American furnishings
from the 1920s through the 1940s,
some carefully refurbished, some
(upstairs) still awaiting rescue.

Judy Naftulin
New Hope, Pennsylvania 18938
215.297.0702
By appointment only. From her
home, Ms. Naftulin sells 18th- to
20th-century antiques—1930s
French art deco furnishings, Italian
furniture, garden items, screens, all
in natural and neutral colors.

Olde Hope Antiques
6465 Route 202
New Hope, Pennsylvania 18938
215.862.5055
Antique American country furniture
and folk art; early painted pieces,
weathervanes, and textiles.

Renningers Extravaganza
740 Noble Street
Kutztown, Pennsylvania 19530
717.385.0104
The Antiques Market every Saturday
features more than 250 booths selling antiques and collectibles; "extrav-
aganzas" in April, June, and
September draw four times as many
dealers.

Weisshouse Design Store
5511 Walnut Street
Pittsburgh, Pennsylvania 15232
412.687.1111
Well-designed home furnishings,
from Mitchell Gold and Shabby Chic
sofas to Eames chairs.

MIDWEST
ILLINOIS

Arts 220
895½ Green Bay Road
Winnetka, Illinois 60093
847.501.3084
Fern Simon stocks furniture and
sculpture by the 20th-century masters: Harry Bertoia, George Nelson,
and Carlo Bugatti.

Chicago Faucets
2100 South Clearwater
Des Plaines, Illinois 60611
847.803.5000
The best place for faucets and fixtures with an architectural feel.

Christa's
217 West Illinois Street
Chicago, Illinois 60610
312.222.2520
A densely stocked antiques shop with silver, glass, porcelain, chairs, and a trove of antique French furniture.

Elements
102 East Oak Street
Chicago, Illinois 60611
312.642.6574
Small home furnishings and tabletop pieces with a hint of Asian, African, and art deco influences.

Fortunate Discoveries
1022 West Armitage Avenue
Chicago, Illinois 60614
773.404.0212
Tribal rugs; carved and painted ethnic furnishings and artifacts.

Golden Triangle
72 West Hubbard Street
Chicago, Illinois 60610
312.755.1266
Reasonably priced furniture, new and antique, from Thailand, Burma, and Laos.

Jay Robert's Antique Warehouse
149 West Kinzie Street
Chicago, Illinois 60610
312.222.0167
Antiques and accessories of every provenance, including turn-of-the-century armoires, beds, and desks from Europe.

Jean Alan
2062 North Damen Avenue
Chicago, Illinois 60647
773.278.2345
A former movie set designer's atelier of draperies, pillows, and Christine Tarkowski's photo-imagery-based wallpapers.

Ligne Roset
56 East Walton Street
Chicago, Illinois 60611
312.867.1207
Comfortable and contemporary French furniture, from sofabeds and shelving to tables and rugs. Also in Seattle and Miami.

Luminaire
301 West Superior Street
Chicago, Illinois 60610
312.664.9582
Furnishings and lighting from the major contemporary European manufacturers, including B&B Italia, Cassina, Montis, Luce Plan, and Flos. Also in Coral Gables, Florida.

Manifesto
755 North Wells Street
Chicago, Illinois 60610
312.664.0733
High-end modern furnishings, including bedroom and dining-room pieces from Promemoria, Minotti, and other Italian firms.

Mig and Tig
549 North Wells Street
Chicago, Illinois 60610
312.644.8277
A lavish mix of furnishings, from wall sconces that hold flowers to velvet-slipcovered sofas. Also chairs, lamps, and custom work. Catalog available; call 800.222.1532.

Northern Possessions
900 North Michigan Avenue
Chicago, Illinois 60611
312.397.0300
From 1,200 artisans come the vases, glassware, lamps, armoires, painted chests, and fantastical beds that stock this store.

Room and Board
Chicago Place
700 North Michigan Avenue
Level 6 & 7
Chicago, Illinois 60611
312.266.0656
The place to find Herman Miller as well as accessible contemporary furniture and lighting.

Salvage One
1524 Sangamon Street
Chicago, Illinois 60608
312.733.0098
Architectural salvage: stained-glass windows, pillars, gates, doors, mantels, some furniture, and cast-iron tubs.

Sawbridge Studios
406 North Clark Street
Chicago, Illinois 60610
312.828.0055
Irish cottage-style furniture—sleighbeds, tables, and dressers—made in Vermont; accessories and furnishings by dozens of artisans.

Shabby Chic
54 East Walton Street
Chicago, Illinois 60611
312.649.0080
Slipcovered furnishings with a squashy, inviting look. Also in Santa Monica, San Francisco, and New York.

Tabula Tua
1015 West Armitage Avenue
Chicago, Illinois 60614
773.525.3500
French country furniture, handmade mosaic tables, custom and artisan-made dinnerware; also glass and pottery from Cyclamen Studio, Dan Levy, and Susan WaRoad.

Urban Gardener
1006 West Armitage Avenue
Chicago, Illinois 60614
312.477.2070
Architectural elements, topiaries, hand-thrown pots, garden furnishings; note the lightweight fiberglass pots for balcony gardeners.

INDIANA

Collections Antiques
111 East 49th Street
Indianapolis, Indiana 46205
317.283.5251
Antiques, accessories, and one-of-a-kind items for the home, particularly 19th-century French and English pieces.

Houseworks
39117 East 82nd Street
Indianapolis, Indiana 46240
317.578.7000
Modern and retro furniture, accessories, and lighting, including frames and mirrors, magazine racks, china, end tables, cocktail tables, and upholstered seating.

Michigan Street Antique Center
1049 East Michigan Avenue
Indianapolis, Indiana 46202
317.972.8990
Vintage Herman Miller and Knoll furniture, and an array of lamps, paintings, rugs, and textiles from the 1930s to the 1960s. Also American antiques; 50 vendors in a 10,000 square feet space.

KANSAS

G. Diebolt's
608 Commercial Street
Atchinson, Kansas 66002
913.367.2395
Products for the inviting bed: linens, pillows, custom-made duvets, shams.

Nell Hill's
501 Commercial Street
Atchinson, Kansas 66002
913.367.1086
An urban mix of furnishings and accessories, from antique French furniture to lighting, frames, and candlesticks.

MICHIGAN

Architectura/In Situ
474 North Old Woodward Avenue
Birmingham, Michigan 48009
248.646.0097
A great source for modern European furniture and accessories.

MINNESOTA

American Island
3505 West 44th Street
Minneapolis, Minnesota 55410
612.925.9006
Furnishings for the garden, handmade birdhouses, and renewed antiques—"comfortable, traditional furniture we can redo and pass along," as partners James Hanson and Steve Douthit put it. Interior design services offered.

Architectural Antiques
801 Washington Avenue, North
Minneapolis, Minnesota 55401
612.332.8344
Architectural salvage and ecclesiastical artifacts from the turn of the century through the 1930s: wrought-iron fences and gates, doors, lighting, chandeliers, mantels, and staircases.

Past Present Future
336 East Franklin Avenue
Minneapolis, Minnesota 55404
612.870.0702
"Open by appointment or by chance." One of the country's largest inventories of vintage office furniture, some of it restored, including cabinets, lamps, and chairs in metal and wood.

MISSOURI

Celadon
401 North Euclid Avenue
St. Louis, Missouri 63108
314.361.7115
The exotic and the beautiful: silk Fortuny lanterns, shell lamps, silk throws, paper twine rugs from Finland, tansu chests made of reclaimed wood from Asian temples, silk pillows adorned with peacock feathers.

Cummings Corner
1703 West 45th Street
Kansas City, Missouri 64111
816.753.5353
Antique and vintage furnishings, including lighting, windows, chests of drawers, folk art tables, garden gates, and urns.

Mossa Center
1214 Washington Avenue
St. Louis, Missouri 63103
314.241.5199
Fine modern European furniture and accessories.

NEBRASKA

Conner's Architectural Antiques
701 P Street
Lincoln, Nebraska 68508
402.435.3338
Antique lighting, stained-glass windows, iron fencing, and woodwork; also antique tableware, including Fostoria and Haviland.

OHIO

Antiques Etcetera Mall
3265 North High Street
Columbus, Ohio 43202
614.447.2242
A cluster of 20 dealers specializing in furniture, pottery, and glass.

Suite Lorain
7105 Lorain Avenue
Cleveland, Ohio 44102
216.281.1959
The 15 dealers here specialize in 1950s furniture, lighting, and accessories. Watch for vintage dinette sets —and also some Heywood Wakefield and Herman Miller.

Voltage, Inc.
2703 Observatory Avenue
Cincinnati, Ohio 45208
513.871.5483
European contemporary furniture and accessories.

Wooden Nickel Architectural Antiques
1410 Central Parkway
Cincinnati, Ohio 45210
513.241.2985
The architectural salvage here includes fancy Victorian furniture, mirrors, stained glass, restored chandeliers, mantels, and garden fountains. Also at 9748 Montgomery Road.

WISCONSIN

Eccola
237 North Broadway
Milwaukee, Wisconsin 53202
414.273.3727
One-of-a-kind and artisan-made furnishings, including tables made from metal grates, custom-designed steel table bases and beds; also clocks, candles, and lamps.

NEW ENGLAND
CONNECTICUT

Cove Landing
248 Hamburg Road, Route 156
Lyme, Connecticut
(mailing address: P.O. Box 39,
Hadlyme, Connecticut, 06439)
860.526.3464
Open Fridays, Saturdays, and by
appointment. Antiques and stylish
objects, from 19th-century Irish,
English, and Russian furnishings to
Ralph Lauren flatware.

The Drapery Exchange
1899 Post Road
Darien, Connecticut 06820
203.655.3844
A consignment shop for pre-owned
curtains, often of lavish materials or
elaborate design. Curtains can be
taken home on approval and altered
through the shop.

Garden House
18 East Shore Road
New Preston, Connecticut 06777
860.868.6790
English, French, and some American
antiques and metal garden furnishings, most with patina or a bit of rust;
urns, birdbaths, statuary, painted furniture, and folk art.

United House Wrecking
535 Hope Street
Stamford, Connecticut 06906
203.348.5371
Connecticut's self-proclaimed largest
antiques store, stocked with chandeliers, mantels, and just about anything that can be plucked from an
old building.

Uproar
336 Elm Street
Westport, Connecticut 06880
203.221.9210
Custom furnishings, created from 70
sofa designs and 500 fabrics; also
armoires, desks, bookcases, beds,
and custom-made iron furniture.

MAINE

Architectural Antiquities
Harborside, Maine 04642
207.326.4938
Doors, brackets, brass lighting fixtures, mantels, columns, slate sinks,
and other objects, from a yard that
also refurbishes and refinishes its
stock.

Green Design Furniture
267 Commercial Street
Portland, Maine 04101
800.853.4234
Mission-style desks, beds, chairs,
and other clean-lined cherry furnishings for the home and home office.
Catalog available.

Maine Cottage Furniture
Lower Falls Landing
106 Lafayette Street
Yarmouth, Maine 04096
207.846.1430
Chairs, tables, shelving, beds, and
other furnishings with cottage appeal,
bright colors, and clean lines, all of
painted wood.

MASSACHUSETTS
Boston and Cambridge

Adesso
200 Boylston Street
Boston, Massachusetts 02116
617.451.2212
The Boston branch of Ligne Roset,
offering modern European lighting
and furniture.

Black Ink at Home
101 Charles Street
Boston, Massachusetts 02114
617.723.3883
Housewares and accessories with a
refined American feel.

Domain
7 Newbury Street
Boston, Massachusetts 02116
617.266.5252
Slipcovered loveseats, chairs, and
sofas; glamorous upholstered and
metal beds, armoires and accessories. Domain has 23 locations
nationally; for information, call
800.888.1388.

F.KIA
558 Tremont Street
Boston, Massachusetts 02118
617.357.5553
Simple, innovative products for the
home: candles, shower curtains, towels, hand-blown vases, bath items for
adults and children.

Henry Solo
35 Newbury Street
Boston, Massachusetts 02116
617.267.3388
Hand-painted Italian and American
pottery, hand-carved chairs, table
linens, plates, frames, throws and
shams, bathroom accessories, and a
great selection of invitations and
stationery.

Industry
276 Newbury Street
Boston, Massachusetts 02116
617.437.0319
Hand-painted lampshades, mosaic
tabletops, lighting fixtures, clocks,
and frames, made in Industry's own
studio. Also in Braintree,
Massachusetts.

JMW Gallery
144 Lincoln Street
Boston, Massachusetts 02111
617.338.9097
Mission furniture, art pottery, and
American Arts and Crafts
accessories.

Lou Lou's Lost & Found
121 Newbury Street
Boston, Massachusetts 02116
617.859.8593
Irresistible travel nostalgia: china, silver, glassware, toastracks, ashtrays,
and more, from grand hotels and
restaurants around the world.

Matsu
237 Newbury Street
Boston, Massachusetts 02116
617.226.9707
Accessories with an Asian sense,
from pens to trays to glassware.

MDF
19 Brattle Street
Cambridge, Massachusetts 02138
617.491.2789
The name stands for Modern
Designer Furnishings: wood and steel
tables, and lamps by George
Raustiala; Cec le Page acrylic candlesticks; and mirrors, vases, and
wood and steel tables by other
artists.

Mohr & McPherson
290 Concord Avenue
Cambridge, Massachusetts 02138
617.354.6662
Reasonably priced hand-crafted furniture and accessories, including
18th- and 19th-century Chinese
antiques and Japanese Tansu chests.
Also at 81 Arlington Street in Boston.

Placewares
160 Newbury Street
Boston, Massachusetts 02116
617.267.5460
The place to get organized.

Repertoire
114 Boylston Street
Boston, Massachusetts 02116
617.426.3865
Style-conscious furnishings and
objects by Philippe Starck, Borek
Sipek, Driade, Rosenthal, Max Alto,
Romeo Sozzi, Flexform, and other
high-profile sources. A designer-
quality showroom open to the public.

Statewide

**Brimfield Antiques and
Collectibles Shows**
Auction Acres, Route 20
Brimfield, Massachusetts 01010
413.245.9556
The largest outdoor show in the
country—4,000 dealers across 20
fields. Held for six days every May,
July, and September.

C'est la Vie
24 Atlantic Avenue
Marblehead, Massachusetts 01945
781.639.2468
One-of-a-kind and custom furnishings, including handmade lamps,
decoupage lampshades, dishware,
antique hand-painted furniture, art
pottery, and china.

**The Country Dining Room
Antiques**
178 Main Street
Great Barrington, Massachusetts
    01230
413.528.5050
Antique china, silver, and glassware,
mostly 18th- and 19th-century
English.

Good Time Stove Co.
188 Cape Street (Route 112)
Goshen, Massachusetts 01032
413.268.3677
Antique wood, coal, and gas stoves,
most dating from 1830 to 1940,
restored (or converted to electric) by
owner Richard Richardson.

Ross Brothers Antiques
28 North Maple Street
Florence, Massachusetts 01062
413.586.3875
Architectural salvage (doors, columns,
gates, windows), used furniture in rustic
and classic styles, and antique boats.

RHODE ISLAND

Richard Kazarian Antiques
325 Water Street
Warren, Rhode Island 02885
401.245.0700
Antiques with patina and character,
for garden and home: urns,
pedestals, 19th-century iron and
bronze outdoor furniture, tapestry-
covered Italian chairs.

NEW YORK
NEW YORK CITY

ABC Carpet & Home
Broadway at East 19th Street
New York, New York 10003
212.473.3000
An extraordinary home-furnishings
emporium, stocked with Italian
damask bed linens, Venetian chandeliers, antique-lacquered Chinese
furniture, handmade Tibetan rugs,
fabric by the yard, French cherry
farm tables, art deco leather club
chairs, and much more.

Ad Hoc Softwares
410 West Broadway
New York, New York 10012
212.925.2652
Clean, modern fine linens and
tableware.

Aero
132 Spring Street
New York, New York 10012
212.966.1500
Even the antique furnishings and
accessories at Aero have a modern
sensibility. Owner Thomas O'Brien's
line of classic 1940s-style furniture is
here, along with pieces by Alvar
Aalto, Donald McKay, and others.

Amalgamated Home
9 Christopher Street
New York, New York 10014
212.255.4160
Everything from spare modern to
over the top.

**The Annex Antique Fair and Flea
Market**
Sixth Avenue at 25th and 26th
    Streets
New York, New York 10001
212.243.5343
Hundreds of dealers, with a sweep-
ing assortment of antiques and vin-
tage finds in outdoor lots and numer-
ous nearby buildings; held every
Saturday and Sunday.

Anthropologie
375 West Broadway
New York, New York 10012
212.343.7070
A range of merchandise with a rustic,
antique feel.

B&B Italia
150 East 58th Street
New York, New York 10155
212.758.4046
Modern Italian furniture from Antonio
Citterio.

Bergdorf Goodman
754 Fifth Avenue
New York, New York 10019
212.753.7300
Everything from classic to the
newest-thing tabletop and
accessories.

British Khaki
62 Greene Street
New York, New York 10012
212.343.2299
British Colonial furniture, mostly wood.

Cassina
155 East 56th Street
New York, New York 10021
212.861.1313
Beautiful modern Italian furniture.

Chelsea Paggage at Barney's New York
660 Madison Avenue
New York, New York 10021
212.833.2066
212.833.2070
Crafty, graphic tabletops, and linens from all over the world.

Cobweb Antiques
116 West Houston Street
New York, New York 10012
212.505.1558
Antiques from Morocco, mostly furniture, also architectural details.

Coconut Company
131 Greene Street
New York, New York 10012
212.539.1940
Furniture imports from all around India.

Crate and Barrel
650 Madison Avenue
New York, New York 10022
212.308.0011
Housewares and furniture.

Dialogica
484 Broome Street
New York, New York 10013
212.966.1934
Modern and sensual furnishings—beds, chairs, vitrines, rugs—designed by Monique and Sergio Savarese. Also at 1070 Madison Avenue and in Los Angeles, San Diego, San Francisco, Chicago, and Boston.

Dykes Lumber Company
348 West 44th Street
New York, New York 10036
212.246.6480
Besides the usual lumber and hardware, Dykes carries a large selection of trims, moldings, table legs, doors, and decorative elements for walls and ceilings. Also in New Jersey.

Escabelle Imports, Ltd.
273 Lafayette Street
New York, New York 10012
212.941.5925
Beautifully edited French vintage wares and antiques.

Felissimo
10 West 56th Street
New York, New York 10019
212.247.1800
Accessories with an Asian feel in a Feng Shui atmosphere.

Form and Function
95 Vandam Street
New York, New York 10013
212.414.1800
Mid-century modern original furniture and accessories.

Gallery 91
91 Grand Street
New York, New York 10013
212.966.3722
Enticing, experimental designs with a whimsical feel.

Global Table
109 Sullivan Street
New York, New York 10012
212.431.5839
Elegant, pared-down tableware from all over the world, with an emphasis on materials.

Golden Oldies
132-29 33rd Avenue
Flushing, New York 11354
800.435.0547
Vast rooms crammed with antique armoires, custom-fitted on request to hold televisions or other storage; also antique mahogany and pine tables and chairs.

Grand Brass Lamp Parts, Inc.
221 Grand Street
New York, New York 10013
212.226.2567
Crystals for chandeliers, old parts for old lamps, vintage-looking electrical cords, and rewiring.

H Store
335 East 9th Street
New York, New York 10003
212.477.2631
An interior designer's notion store of furniture and accessories.

Henri Bendel
712 Fifth Avenue
New York, New York 10019
212.247.1100
Opulent, crafty tableware and accessories.

ICF (International Contract Furnishings)
305 East 63rd Street
New York, New York 10021
212.388.1000
Reissues of iconic 20th-century furniture, as well as new designs.

Interieurs
114 Wooster Street
New York, New York 10012
212.343.0800
A well-edited selection of antiques, contemporary furniture, textiles, lamps, and accessories from the South of France. The homemade candles weigh up to 200 pounds.

Irreplaceable Artifacts
14 Second Avenue
New York, New York 10003
212.777.2900
Antique fireplaces, stone and terracotta ornaments, doors, plumbing, and other architectural salvage.

Knoll International
105 Wooster Street
New York, New York 10012
212.343.4000
The best of the Bauhaus through Maya Lin's new line, also textiles.

Lee's Lighting
1755 Broadway
New York, New York 10019
212.581.4400
A good selection of lighting from
Europe and the U.S.

Lin Weinberg
84 Wooster Street
New York, New York 10012
212.219.3022
Mid-century modern collectible pieces.

Lost City Arts
275 Lafayette Street
New York, New York 10012
212.941.8025
Mid-century modern furniture and
accessories, and reissues of Warre.

Modernage/Cappellini
102 Wooster Street
New York, New York 10012
212.966.0669
A complete presentation of Cappellini
furniture as well as rugs by Christine
Van Der Hurd.

MoMA Store
11 West 53rd Street
New York, New York 10019
212.708.9700
Museum of Modern Art's store for
reproduction architect furniture, lighting, and accessories, as well as their
own designs.

Moss
146 Greene Street
New York, New York 10012
212.226.2190
Mid-century and industrial furniture,
lighting, and accessories; Kartell's
transparent plastic storage units; Ingo
Maurer lighting.

Mxyplyzyk
125 Greenwich Avenue
New York, New York 10014
212.989.4300
Functionally designed accessories for
home and office.

Palazzetti
515 Madison Avenue
New York, New York 10022
212.832.1199
Popularly priced adaptations of modern classics.

Portico
72 Spring Street
New York, New York 10012
212.941.7800
Clean, elegant, comfortable furnishings and accessories.

Rhubarb Home
26 Bond Street
New York, New York 10012
212.533.1817
Farmhouse furnishings and objects
of whimsical design—painted chairs,
cabinets, iron beds—from Mexico,
Central America, and the owner's
Ohio hometown. Also custom-
designed home furnishings and dog
beds.

Roche Bobois
200 Madison Avenue
New York, New York 10016
212.889.5304
French contemporary design.

Rooms & Gardens
290 Lafayette Street
New York, New York 10012
212.431.1297
Owner Margaret Rubino's collection
of 19th- and early 20th-century
French antiques for home and garden, including antique store fixtures,
drapers' tables, zinc-framed mirrors,
and gueridon tables.

S. A. Bendheim Company
122 Hudson Street
New York, New York 10013
212.226.6370
Hand-blown glass for window restoration: panes with pockmarks, bubbles,
and varying degrees of distortion. Art
and architectural glass; classes
offered on stained glass.

Salon Moderne
281 Lafayette Street
New York, New York 10012
212.219.3439
Modern Italian upholstered furniture,
accessories, and tables and chairs.

See Ltd.
920 Broadway
New York, New York 10010
212.288.3600
Everything from beds to flatware, with
a hard edge.

Shì
233 Elizabeth Street
New York, New York 10012
212.334.2392
Lighting, ceramics, and small pieces
of furniture, mainly French-designed.

Simon's Hardware
421 Third Avenue
New York, New York 10016
212.532.9220
A massive selection of designer-
friendly hardware.

Smith & Hawkin
394 West Broadway
New York, New York 10012
212.925.0867
Classic garden furniture and English
garden tools.

Takashimaya
693 Fifth Avenue
New York, New York 10022
212.350.0100
Boutique department store focusing
on Asian display, with everything
from travel accessories to bento
lunch boxes.

Terra Verde
120 Wooster Street
New York, New York 10012
212.925.4533
Ecological tableware, furniture,
linens, and accessories.

Time Will Tell
962 Madison Avenue
New York, New York 10021
212.861.2663
Vintage collectible watches and clocks.

Totem Design Group
71 Franklin Street
New York, New York 10013
212.925.5506
Innovative furniture from young
designers including Karim Rashid,
Gaston Marticorena, Ross Menuez,
Nick Dine, and Harry Allen.

Treillage
418 East 75th Street
New York, New York 10021
212.525.2288
Cement and iron garden furniture.

Troy
138 Greene Street
New York, New York 10012
212.941.4777
A minimalist, 8000-square-foot
gallery of home furnishings, including
furniture by Arne Jacobsen and Arne
Alto; V'Soske rugs and pieces by the
owner, Troy Halterman.

Urban Archaeology
285 Lafayette Street
New York, New York 10012
212.431.6969
Architectural elements from bal-
lustrades to stained glass windows.

Waterworks
469 Broome Street
New York, New York 10012
212.966.0605
Tubs and sinks to fixtures with a classic European feel. Also, furniture by
Aero.

**Whitney Museum's Store Next
Door**
943 Madison Avenue
New York, New York 10021
212.606.0200
Selection of craft pieces by artists.

Wyeth
151 Franklin Street
New York, New York 10013
212.925.5278
Modern classics and unusual vintage
furnishings by American and
European designers, with an emphasis on materials (stainless steel, old
rattan) and an industrial aesthetic.

Statewide

The Front Porch
309 Main Street
Port Washington, New York 11050
516.944.6868
Used furniture and antiques.

Great American Antiquefest
Phoenix, New York
315.695.6115
More than 500 dealers gather here
annually, on the third weekend of
every July.

Home Depot Expo Design Center
1250 Corporate Drive
Westbury, New York 11590
516.222.0990
A domestic superstore packed with
velvet pillows, French chairs, bed
linens, decorative planters, architectural relics, tile, carpet, custom framing, hundreds of fabrics, even a
sewing service. Also in Atlanta,
Dallas, San Diego, Miami, and
Davies, Florida.

Oster-Jensen Art and Antiques
86 Birch Hill Road
Locust Valley, New York 11560
516.676.5454
Chests, mirrors, and other good
English and American antiques.

**Raymond Knight Antiques and KII
Designs**
121 Birch Hill Road
Locust Valley, New York 11560
516.671.7046
Antiques and reproductions: furniture, porcelain, sterling silver pieces,
tableware.

Ruby Beets Antiques
1703 Montauk Highway
Bridgehampton, New York 11932
516.537.2802
A 12-room house stocked with painted furniture, Victorian upholstered
seating, quirky vintage finds, and
nonpedigreed pieces from the early
1800s to 1960. A favorite among
New York decorators.

Schwartz's Forge and Metalworks
2695 Route 315
Deansboro, New York 13328
315.841.4477
Custom architectural metalwork: stair
railings, entry doors, wrought-iron
fences, balustrades.

NORTHWEST
OREGON

Twist
30 Northwest 23rd Place
Portland, Oregon 97210
503.224.0334
American crafts with a contemporary
design edge. Blown glass, scrap-
metal sculptures, ceramics, hand-
carved furnishings by more than 200
artisans.

Urbino
521 Northwest 23rd Avenue
Portland, Oregon 97210
503.220.0053
Accessories for tabletop and bath:
soap, candles, ceramics, dinnerware,
glassware, and more. A sister shop,
Urbino Home, sells upholstered and
slipcovered furniture—including
Shabby Chic—and bed linens at 738
Northwest 23rd Avenue,
503.220.4194.

WASHINGTON

Andrews and Arnold
86 Pine Street
Seattle, Washington 98101
206.443.4230
A mix of new and antique: old bamboo shelves and chairs, Simon
Pearce glassware, fishing baskets,
old English flatware, and candles and
frames.

Bitters Co.
513 North 36th Street
Seattle, Washington 98103
206.632.0886
Imported and antique furnishings;
the stock, unpredictable, and engag-
ing, ranges from Indonesian storage
cabinets to antique Chilean cooking
pots.

Collectors III
Seattle, Washington
By appointment: 206.522.6638
Antique furnishings and decorative
objects from England—"whatever is
old, good, and reasonably priced,"
says partner Elaine Bosworth.

Current
1201 Western Avenue
Seattle, Washington 98101
206.622.2433
The Seattle source for European contemporary furniture and accessories.

David Smith & Company
334 Boren Avenue North
Seattle, Washington 98109
206.223.1598
"An excellent source for Indonesian antiques, including beautiful dining tables and unusual chairs and garden furniture," writes Humphrey. Also daybeds, cabinets, and armoires.

Domestic Furniture
1422 34th Avenue
Seattle, Washington 98122
206.323.0198
Roy McMakin's wood and upholstered furniture—supremely simple, slightly overscaled; some pieces evoke memories of schoolhouse chairs and other furniture icons from the past. Also custom furnishings.

The Environmental Home Center
1724 Fourth Avenue South
Seattle, Washington 98134
206.682.7332
A 9,000-square-foot warehouse stocked with recycled lumber; chemical-free mattresses; nontoxic paints, finishes, and building materials; granitelike countertops made from soy-flour oil; even environmentally friendly sheets.

A Garden of Distinction
5819 Sixth Avenue South
Seattle, Washington 98108
206.763.0517
Garden ornaments, vintage tools, and antique iron gates; garden furniture made from reclaimed barn siding, and imports from all over the world.

Glenn Richards
964 Denny Way
Seattle, Washington 98109
206.287.1877
Sideboards, kitchen chests, stone lanterns, and other furnishings from China, Japan, India, Indonesia, and the Philippines.

Great Jones Home
1921 Second Avenue
Seattle, Washington 98101
206.448.9405
Primitive 19th- and 20th-century antiques, California pottery, linens, and down-filled, slipcovered furniture. The owners describe their aesthetic as "genteel and humble."

NIDO
1920½ First Avenue
Seattle, Washington 98101
206.443.1272
"Small but perfect accessories and found objects," writes Humphreys. Lighting, small furniture, brass beds, petite cabinets, antiques from England and France.

Pande Cameron
815 Pine Street
Seattle, Washington 98101
206.624.6263
Decorative and antique rugs in traditional Oriental designs; Tibetan and Nepalese rugs; custom designs.

Sur La Table
84 Pine Street
Seattle, Washington 98101
800.243.0852
Call for additional locations; tableware from France, including beautiful copper pots and pans.

SOUTH
ALABAMA

Bodiford's Antique Mall
7834 Troy Highway
Pike Road, Alabama 36064
334.280.3620
A 100-year-old house-turned-store, stocked with Victorian, primitive, and English antiques.

The Elegant Earth
1907 Cahaba Road
Birmingham, Alabama 35223
205.870.3264
Antique and vintage garden furnishings from many countries: benches, lanterns, urns, finials, gates, pedestals, wall plaques.

FLORIDA

American Salvage
7001 and 9200 Northwest 27th
   Avenue
Miami, Florida 33147
305.691.7001 and 305.836.4444
In two locations, a total of 85,000 square feet of columns, grillework, doors, chandeliers, vintage toilets, and furniture.

Berkley Floral Supply Co.
2360 Northwest 23rd Street
Miami, Florida 33172
305.638.4141
"Where the floral designers shop—for flowers, plants, ribbons, candles, and more," writes *Met Home* city editor Nisi Berryman.

Boca Bargoons
15801 South Dixie Highway
Miami, Florida 33157
305.255.1718
Upholstery and drapery fabrics, many discontinued from Clarence House, Brunschwig & Fils, Cowtan & Tout, all at unusually good prices.

Braun & Trujillo
1042 East 27th Street
Hialeah, Florida 33013
305.696.0623
Finials and curtain rods in rustic, hand-worked metal, from stock designs like arrows and sunbursts to custom pieces.

Details
1031 Lincoln Road
Miami Beach, Florida 33139
305.531.1325
Half the store holds American contemporary design, the other half stocks rustic, old-world furnishings. Throughout: framed art, tabletop pieces, beds, armoires, rugs. Also in Coral Gables.

Florida Victorian Architectural Salvage
112 West Georgia Avenue
Deland, Florida 32720
904.734.9300
25,000 square feet of doors, windows, columns, wall hangings, garden benches, iron gates, antique bricks, and beams, plus hand-built custom furniture.

Joseph's Antiques & Things
515 Fleming Street
Key West, Florida 33040
305.292.1333
Many nautical antiques, including lamps, prints, glassware, books, and bottles.

Miami Twice
6562 Southwest 40th Street
Miami, Florida 33155
305.669.9143
"A wild array of vintage furniture, with fast moving stock," writes Nisi Berryman.

Morgenstern's
2520 Coral Way, Suite 2306
Miami, Florida 33145
By appointment only:
305.854.2744
Antique rugs, furnishings, paintings, and pottery; modern paintings by Latin American and Cuban artists.

Neo Studio
3841 Northeast Second Avenue
Suite 202
Miami, Florida 33137
305.438.9500
Twentieth-century classics: chairs by Gio Ponti, tables by T.H. Robsjohn-Gibbings, vases by Archimede Seguso, and contemporary furniture lines like Hugues Chevalier and Hassan Abouseda.

Senzatempo
1655 Meridian Avenue
Miami Beach, Florida 33139
305.534.5588
Mid-century modern furniture, lighting, and decorative objects; also jewelry and pens.

Valerio Antiques
2901 Florida Avenue, Suite 806
Coconut Grove, Florida 33133
305.448.6779
French art deco furniture, including desks, end tables, bronze and ivory figures, and dining sets; also Lalique glass.

Well Design
6550 Southwest 40th Street
Miami, Florida 33155
305.661.1386
Furniture and objects with a 1960s affinity; lots of chrome and Lucite.

Peter Werner
3709 South Dixie Highway
West Palm Beach, Florida 33405
561.832.0428
Twentieth-century furniture and objects, "all picked with a twisted connoisseur's eye," writes Berryman. "Eccentric and wonderful."

Yardware
1021 Lincoln Road
Miami Beach, Florida 33139
305.531.2002
Stylish gardenware, tools, vases, garden books, and accessories.

GEORGIA

Atlanta Antiques Exchange
1185 Howell Mill Road, Northwest
Atlanta, Georgia 30318
404.351.0727
Specializes in English, Continental, and Asian ceramics and decorative accessories: lamps, vases, platters, planters, and candlesticks.

Ballard's Backroom
1670 Defoor Avenue, Northwest
Atlanta, Georgia 30318
404.352.2776
A warehouse of overstocked and discontinued furnishings and accessories from the lavish Ballard Designs Catalog, with savings of up to 80 percent.

Curry & Co.
200 Ottley Drive, Northeast
Atlanta, Georgia 30324
404.885.1444
Lighting and furniture manufacturer.

Domus
6438 Dawson Boulevard
Norcross, Georgia 30093
404.448.4913
Modern European furniture and accessories.

Interiors Market
55 Bennett Street, Northwest
No. 20
Atlanta, Georgia 30309
404.352.0055
From 45 dealers, a mix of mirrors, porcelain, English chests, pine tables and armoires, silver serving pieces, and Victorian bamboo tables.

Lush Life
145 East Andrews Drive
Atlanta, Georgia 30305
404.841.9661
Amid the plants are new and antique gardening accessories, French planters and confit pots, lamps, objects from the Paris flea markets, candles, linens, and soaps.

Sandy Springs Galleries
233 Hildebrand Drive, Northeast
Atlanta, Georgia 30328
404.252.3244
Hundreds of glittering chandeliers and sconces, circa 1850–1930.

LOUISIANA

Albany Woodworks
30380 Payne Alley
Albany, Louisiana 70711
504.567.1155
Antique (reclaimed) building materials, including heart-cypress and heart-pine flooring; also custom-made flooring, paneling, shutters, and doors.

Angéle Parlange Design
5419 Magazine Street
New Orleans, Louisiana 70115
504.897.6511
"Parlange fuses historical precedents from her French ancestry—such as fleur-de-lis and crown motifs—with her own modern wit and style when creating fabrics, pillows, and furniture," writes Ellen Johnson.

Anne Pratt Designs
3937 Magazine Street
New Orleans, Louisiana 70115
504.891.6532
Ecclesiastical and other objects from Mexico: church candelabras, crucifixes, tin frames, milagros (small silver images of body parts, offered to saints for healing), and ceramics.

Antiques de Provence
708 East Boston Street
Covington, Louisiana 70433
504.875.0087
French country antiques, including beds, armoires, hand-carved limestone fountains, French farm tables, and trumeaux.

The Curtain Exchange
3947 Magazine Street
New Orleans, Louisiana 70118
504.897.2444
Previously owned draperies, blinds, and shades, sold on consignment, that would cost much more if new; from $25 to $1,500 per window. The shop also designs and makes custom window treatments. Franchises opening in Baton Rouge, Dallas, Atlanta, and other cities.

GB
3806 Magazine Street, Suite 3
New Orleans, Louisiana 70115
504.899.0212
Modern furnishings inspired by classical designs, including creamy-white tables, lamps, and other furniture from the New Magazine Collection designed by Gerrie Bremermann.

J. Schneider's
3806 Magazine Street
New Orleans, Louisiana 70115
504.891.7751
A worthy mix of vintage, modern, and antique furniture; "lots of no-name pieces collected in France, dating from the 1930s," writes city editor Ellen Johnson.

Lucullus
610 Chartres Street
New Orleans, Louisiana 70130
504.528.9620
Patrick Dunne's well-known collection of culinary antiques—from French provincial chairs, tables, and armoires to silver, porcelain, serving utensils, even antique paintings suitable for the dining room.

Mario Villa Gallery
3908 Magazine Street
New Orleans, Louisiana 70115
800.783.8003
Neoclassical metal furnishings designed by Mario Villa, whose work is in prestigious private and public collections. His store also carries upholstered furniture, paintings, photography, and decorative objects. Also in Chicago.

Mirror Mirror
301 Chartres Street
New Orleans, Louisiana 70130
504.566.1990
Antique mirrors, new mirrors in antique frames, mirrored sconces, and found objects (like an old metal washtub) transformed into mirrors.

Necessities
832 Baronne Street
New Orleans, Louisiana 70113
504.581.2333
"Becky Gottsegen's home furnishings gallery specializes in hand-crafted furniture, lighting, and fabrics from the city's best artisans and designers," writes *Met Home* city editor Ellen Johnson.

Pied Nu
5521 Magazine Street
New Orleans, Louisiana 70115
504.899.4118
Owner Sallee Benjamin's intriguing assortment of modern home furnishings and women's accessories. (The name means "barefoot" in French.)

MARYLAND

Annapolis Antiques & Consignment Mall
20 Riverview Avenue
Annapolis, Maryland 21401
410.266.5550
From about 30 dealers, a mix of mahogany, Victorian, oak, pine, and mid-century furniture; also glassware, garden items, watercolors, and oil paintings.

Chesapeake Antique Center
6527 Friels Road
Queenstown, Maryland 21658
410.827.6640
A 10,000-square-foot building packed with individual dealers, who sell home furnishings and *objets* from the 18th, 19th, and 20th centuries, mostly at reasonable prices.

Firehouse Antiques
102 North Main Street
Galena, Maryland 21635
410.648.5639
Off the beaten path, but a worthwhile source for good 17th- and 18th-century furnishings, rugs, unusual pieces, even some modern furniture.

NORTH CAROLINA

By-Gone Days Antiques
3100 South Boulevard
Charlotte, North Carolina 28209
704.527.8717
Architectural salvage, from doors and fences to mantels and lighting fixtures. Glass tabletops on architectural bases are the only contemporary pieces.

Circa
2321 Crescent Avenue
Charlotte, North Carolina 28207
704.332.1668
European antiques, porcelains, fabrics, and wallcoverings.

SOUTH CAROLINA

Bauer International
455 Long Point Road
Mount Pleasant, South Carolina 29464
803.884.4007
Teak plantation furniture, antiques, and reproductions from the East and West Indies, and a collection of handmade steamer trunks.

Metropolitan Deluxe
164 Market Street
Charleston, South Carolina 29401
803.722.0436
Formerly Maddix Deluxe, this home-furnishings emporium sells ready-made and custom slipcovered furnishings in all styles, from comfortably rumpled to elegant and formal. Also in Georgia and Alabama.

Verve
1127 Gregg Street
Columbia, South Carolina 29201
803.799.0045
Designer Ford Boyd Bailey's collection of furnishings and accessories, with a focus on New Orleans designers: Angéle Parlange (fabrics), Mario Villa (metal furniture), Charles Bohn (pottery).

TENNESSEE

Antique Merchants
2015 Eighth Avenue South
Nashville, Tennessee 37204
615.292.7811
Antique furnishings, silver, crystal, porcelain; furniture from the 1920s; and about 15,000 old or rare books.

Fever
113 South Gay Street
Knoxville, Tennessee 37902
423.525.4771
Twentieth-century classics: beds, desks, tables, and chairs designed by architects; Herman Miller pieces.

Flashback
2304 Central Avenue
Memphis, Tennessee 38104
901.272.2304
A "vintage department store" stocked with Herman Miller, Heywood Wakefield, Austrian art deco armoires, and other mid-century furnishings; also some new furniture.

Pinch Antique Mall
430 North Front Street
Memphis, Tennessee 38103
901.525.0929
Forty-eight antique dealers in the Pinch historic district.

VIRGINIA

Daniel Donnelly Decorative Arts
107 North Fayette Street
Alexandria, Virginia 22314
703.549.4672
Classic modern furniture, including bedroom and dining sets, from Herman Miller, Haywood Wakefield, and other famous makers. Also custom finishes and upholstery for period pieces.

WASHINGTON, D.C.

The Brass Knob Warehouse
2329 Champlain Street, Northwest
Washington, D.C. 20009
202.265.0587
Architectural salvage on a large scale: "house parts," tubs, radiators, sinks, columns, ironwork. A smaller shop at 2311 18th Street, Northwest (202.332.3370), carries doorknobs, lighting fixtures, and mantels.

Marston Luce
1314 21st Street, Northwest
Washington, D.C. 20036
202.775.9460
French country furnishings with original paint; mirrors, lamps, and architectural items for the home and garden.

Mobili
2201 Wisconsin Avenue, Northwest
Washington, D.C. 20007
202.337.2100
European contemporary furniture and accessories.

Oliver Dunn
1657 Wisconsin Avenue, Northwest
Washington, D.C. 20007
202.338.7410
Antique European garden furniture, antique prints, and conservation framing; also antique French and Scandinavian chairs, desks, tables, cabinets, and mirrors.

Theodore's
2233 Wisconsin Avenue, Northwest
Washington, D.C. 20007
202.333.2300 or 800.710.2300
Stylish sofas, chairs, tables, and cabinetry by makers like Directional, Planum, and Della Robbia. Interior design services offered.

TEXAS AND THE SOUTHWEST
ARIZONA

Casa del Encanto
6939 East First Avenue
Scottsdale, Arizona 85251
602.970.1355
Spanish Colonial home furnishings: overscaled iron chairs and lighting fixtures, mahogany and walnut tables, hand-carved stone columns, upholstered furniture, and accessories from Europe and Mexico.

Do Wah Diddy
3642 East Thomas Road
Phoenix, Arizona 85018
602.957.3874
Mid-century modern pieces: lamps, tables, collectibles, and pop culture items from the 1930s through the 1970s.

Extras
3149 East Lincoln Drive
Phoenix, Arizona 85016
602.381.8089
Contemporary tableware, table linens, and unusual decorative items for the dining room.

The Hand and the Spirit Crafts Gallery
4222 North Marshall Way
Scottsdale, Arizona 85253
602.945.8212
"The best fine crafts gallery in the Southwest for contemporary furniture, pots, jewelry, objects, and art," writes Met Home city editor Pam Hait.

Hubbell Trading Post
Highway 264
(mailing address: P.O. Box 388)
Ganado, Arizona 86505
520.755.3254
"Best place in the world to buy Navajo rugs, new and old," writes Hait. "A historic treasure to visit."

Mesquite Grove Gallery
371 McKeown Avenue
(mailing address: P.O. Box 772)
Patagonia, Arizona 85624
520.394.2358
Sculpture for the house and garden; pottery, ironwork, and other artisan-made pieces.

Randall's Linens & Gifts
5919 Cavanaugh Boulevard
Little Rock, Arizona 72207
501.664.1008
Luxury linens include Palais Royale, Frette, and Anichini; also an interesting and wide range of bath products and accessories.

Scottsdale Center for the Arts Gift Shop
7380 East Second Street
Scottsdale, Arizona 85251
602.874.4644
This museum gift shop is known for its works by regional artisans: Damien Velasquez's stainless steel candlesticks, Bill Kasper's art glass, Steven McGovney's ceramic teapots, and hand-painted, Southwestern-style tables by Hoda Das.

ValeriAnne
6922 East Main Street
Scottsdale, Arizona 85251
602.946.8772
Exquisite linens and pillows; accessories and gifts for the home.

COLORADO

Cry Baby Ranch
51422 Larimer Street
Denver, Colorado 80202
303.623.3979
Home furnishings with a Western feel.

Dakota
317 East Colorado Avenue
Telluride, Colorado 81435
970.728.4204
Artisan-made glass, ceramics, and dinnerware; also furnishings of country pine and wicker; upholstered pieces, and unusual lighting fixtures.

Eron Johnson Antiques
451 North Broadway
Denver, Colorado 80203
303.777.8700
A warehouse of 18th- and 19th-century European antiques and accessories, including bookcases, sideboards, and bureaus; garden accessories, iron gates, and a restoration shop on the premises.

Grandpa Snazzy's Antique Hardware
1832 South Broadway
Denver, Colorado 80210
303.777.9264
Crystal doorknobs, drawer pulls, window hardware, door plates, cast-iron hinges, and other fittings—all antique.

Popular Culture
1150 South Broadway
Denver, Colorado 80210
303.777.1163
Furnishings and fine art from the Arts and Crafts period through the 1990s. Italian designs, art deco bedroom sets, mid-century classics by George Nelson and Harry Bertoioa.

Squisito
2628 Third Avenue
Denver, Colorado 80206
303.331.8080
Unusual or artisan-made works for the home: stained-glass fireplace screens, dinnerware, and small furnishings.

NEW MEXICO

Jackalope
2820 Cerrillos Road
Santa Fe, New Mexico 87501
505.471.8539
A gallery of artisan-made objects and furnishings: almirahs (teak armoires), old trunks, and elaborately hand-painted furniture from India; also imports from Mexico, Africa, China, and South America. Other locations in Bernalillo, New Mexico, and Parker, Colorado.

The Natural Choice
1365 Rufina Circle
Santa Fe, New Mexico 87505
800.621.2591
Natural and nontoxic paints, stains, and other finishes, as well as cleaners. Catalog available.

Seret & Sons
224 Galisteo Street
Santa Fe, New Mexico 87501
505.988.9151
Custom-made sofas and chairs; also armoires, tables, and beds made from antique artifacts. Rare kilims, antique architectural pieces, and inlaid marble tables and benches.

Taos Furniture
1807 Second Street, No. 100
Santa Fe, New Mexico 87505
505.988.1229
Hand-crafted Southwestern furnishings—traditional, contemporary, and custom—all made on site.

TEXAS

Adkins Architectural Antiques
3515 Fannin Street
Houston, Texas 77004
713.522.6547 and 800.522.6547
Architectural salvage, including mantels, doors, lighting, plumbing fixtures, even entire balconies.

Architerra
1701 Evergreen Avenue, Suite 2
Austin, Texas 78704
512.441.8062
Terra-cotta and handmade tile imported from Mexico, Portugal, India, and other countries; artist-made tile from all over the United States; hearths and mantels; and custom tile.

Brumder Ornamental Iron
40128 Industrial Park
Georgetown, Texas 78626
512.869.2830
Custom ironwork for interior and exterior use: handrails, gates, doors, tables, chairs, beds, and lighting fixtures.

Dreyfus Antiques Brocante
1901 North Lamar Street
Austin, Texas 78705
512.473.2191
French 18th- and 19th-century country armoires, chairs, tables, hutches, and more, most in walnut or cherry. Also at 719 East Sixth Street (same phone).

Durham Trading & Design Co.
1009 West Sixth Street
Austin, Texas 78703
512.476.1216
American and English antiques and rugs; design services available.

East and Orient Co.
1123 Slocum Street
Dallas, Texas 75207
214.741.1191
Seventeenth- and 18th-century European furniture, porcelain, rugs, and art.

The Fan Man
1914 Abrams Parkway
Dallas, Texas 75214
214.826.7700
New and restored antique and vintage fans from the 1890s on. Catalog available.

Gardens
1818 West 35th Street
Austin, Texas 78703
512.451.5490
"A fabulous nursery also known for
its cutting-edge selection of home
accessories," writes *Met Home* city
editor Helen Thompson.

James Powell Antiques
715 West Avenue
Austin, Texas 78701
512.477.9939
"An incredible shop crammed with
delectable antiques," writes Helen
Johnson. Designers come here for
Venetian, Baroque, and Spanish
Colonial furniture and accessories.

Lars Stanley
2007 Kinney
Austin, Texas 78704
512.445.0444
Architectural metalwork: lighting, fireplace accessories, entry gates, stair
railings, gazebos, and benches; also
candlesticks and other small items.

Legacy Trading Co.
2800 Routh Street, Suite 150
Dallas, Texas 75201
214.953.2222
Frames, candles, a large selection of
upholstered furnishings, and bed
linens in velvet and vintage cloth.
Interior design services available.
Also in Fort Worth.

Nuvo
3900 Cedar Springs Road
Dallas, Texas 75219
214.522.6886
Home furnishings and gifts, with an
emphasis on beds and linens; also
frames, candles, and bath products.

Peacock Alley Retail Store
3210 Armstrong Avenue
Dallas, Texas 75205
214.520.6736
High-end Portuguese bedding,
Egyptian cotton towels and sheets,
down comforters, and other linens for
bed and bath.

Point Five
2444 Times, Suite 100A
Houston, Texas 77005
713.529.5550
Joseph Gregg's collection of Herman
Miller, Knoll, and "all the great fifties
stuff," writes Helen Thompson.

Quatrine Washable Furniture
3120 Knox Street
Dallas, Texas 75205
214.522.2214
Well-made sofas, chairs, and other
upholstered pieces, all with machine-
washable slipcovers. Also in
Manhattan Beach, California;
Houston; Chicago; Detroit; and other
cities.

Radio Ranch
1610 West 35th Street
Austin, Texas 78703
512.459.6855
Reclaimed and polished-up medical
and scientific instruments, cabinets,
and lamps.

**Rolston & Bonick Antiques for the
Garden**
2905 North Henderson Avenue
Dallas, Texas 75206
214.826.7775
Urns, gardening benches and tables,
statuary, antique windows, and
botanical prints. *Met Home* city editor Diane Carroll loves the courtyard
setting, complete with fountain.

Settlers Hardware Company
1901 West Alabama Street
Houston, Texas 77098
713.524.2417
Hinges, drawer pulls, and keyhole
covers are part of this hardware
bonanza, including pieces salvaged
from Texas settlers' buildings.

Whit Hanks Antiques
1009 West 6th Street
Austin, Texas 78703
512.478.2101
A huge selection of rugs, pots,
Indonesian furniture, French and
English antiques, and Colonial
Spanish pieces. Many dealers rent
space here; check out Interior
Imports for Javanese benches and
Dutch Colonial chairs. Also: Whit
Hanks Consignment at 1214 West
Sixth Street, Suite 120,
512.478.2398.

MET HOME'S TOP DESIGN RESOURCES: National and mail order.

SERVICES BY MAIL

*Metal plating and refinishing, particu-
larly for old doorknobs, lighting fixtures, and faucets:*
Hygrade Polishing and Plating Co.
2207 41st Avenue
Long Island City, New York 11101
718.392.4082

CATALOGS

Baggot Leaf Company
430 Broome Street
New York, New York 10013
212.431.GOLD
A catalog of gold- and metal-leafing
supplies, for beginners and experts.
(Classes also offered on site.)

Helen Foster Stencils
71 Main Street
Sanford, Maine 04073
207.490.2625
Stencils based on Arts and Crafts
motifs.

Janovic/Plaza's Incomplete Catalog for Decorative and Scenic Painters
30-35 Thomson Avenue
Long Island City, New York 11101
718.786.4444 in New York City;
800.772.4381 outside
An immense catalog, with tools for faux finishes, ceiling medallions, embossed wallcoverings, and more.

Liz's Antique Hardware
800.939.9003
The mail-order division of a Los Angeles shop overflowing with 350,000 pieces of hardware, including 1940s Bakelite drawer pulls.

Maine Cottage Furniture
207.846.1430
Simple and sturdy furnishings, some with clean lines and some with a country flavor; all of painted wood.

The Natural Choice
1365 Rufina Circle
Santa Fe, New Mexico 87505
800.621.2591
Nontoxic and natural stains, paints, and other products.

Pearl Paint Company
308 Canal Street
New York, New York 10013
800.451.PEARL
A vast selection of supplies for artists, including decorative painters.

Shades of Light
5609F Patterson Avenue
Richmond, Virginia 23226
800.262.6612
Lamps, hanging lanterns, sconces, and chandeliers.

Tassel Time
1249 Stirling Road
Dania, Florida 33004
800.294.6677
Tassels, trimmings, and tiebacks.

V. & Olga Decorating Company
159 Beach 123rd Street
Rockaway Park, New York 11694
718.634.4415
Stencils of moldings, borders, medallions, rosettes, and other architectural ornaments.

PHOTOGRAPHY AND PRODUCTION CREDITS

CALIFORNIA pages 12–17: photographs by Tim Street-Porter; produced by Linda O'Keeffe. • 18–21: photographs by Antoine Bootz; produced by Donna Warner and Donna Paul. • 22–25: photographs by David Phelps; produced by Linda O'Keeffe. • 26–31: photographs by Tim Street-Porter; produced by Newell Turner and Denise Domergue. • 32–33: photographs by John Vaughan; produced by Diane Dorrans Saeks. • 34–37: photographs by Michael Mundy; produced by Diane Dorrans Saeks. • 38–45: photographs by Grey Crawford; produced by Newell Turner. • 46–51: photographs by Jack Winston; produced by Diane Dorrans Saeks.

NORTHWEST pages 54–59: photographs by Michael Skott; produced by Linda O'Keeffe and Linda Humphrey. • 60–63: photographs by Michael Skott; produced by Linda Humphrey and David Staskowski. • 64–67: photographs by Jack Winston; produced by Christopher Hirsheimer and Linda Humphrey.

MIDWEST pages 70–79: photographs by Michael Luppino; produced by Linda O'Keeffe and Lisa Cicotte. • 80–81: photographs by Langdon Clay. • 82–87: photographs by Michael Luppino; produced by Victoria Lautman. • 88–95: photographs by Michael Luppino; produced by Linda O'Keeffe and Lisa Cicotte.

TEXAS AND THE SOUTHWEST pages 98–103: photographs by John Vaughan; produced by Donna Warner and Mindy Pantiel. • 104–9: photographs by Gross & Daley; produced by Newell Turner and Susan Weinberger. • 110–13: photographs by Dominique Vorillon; produced by Christopher Hirsheimer and Pam Hait. • 114–21: photographs by Langdon Clay; produced by Timothy J. Ward and Susan Weinberger. • 122–27: photographs by Dominique Vorillon; produced by Newell Turner and Susan Weinberger. • 128–35: photographs by Grey Crawford; produced by Newell Turner and Susan Weinberger.

SOUTH pages 138–41: photographs by Steven Brooke; produced by Timothy J. Ward and Nisi Berryman. • 142–45: photographs by Dominique Vorillon; produced by Newell Turner. • 146–51: photographs by Steven Brooke; produced by Timothy J. Ward and Vanessa Murphy.

MID-ATLANTIC pages 154–59: photographs by Langdon Clay; produced by Christopher Hirsheimer. • 160–67: photographs by Antoine Bootz; produced by Linda O'Keeffe. • 168–73: photographs by Antoine Bootz; produced by Linda O'Keeffe and Hilary Jay. • 174–79: photographs by Peter Mauss; produced by Newell Turner.

NEW YORK pages 182–83: photographs by Thibault Jeanson; produced by Timothy J. Ward. • 184–93: photographs by Langdon Clay; produced by Linda O'Keeffe. • 194–99: photographs by Michael Luppino; produced by Timothy J. Ward. • 200–205: photographs by Langdon Clay; produced by Donna Warner and David Staskowski. • 206–9: photographs by William Waldron; produced by Newell Turner. • 210–15: photographs by Peter Estersohn. • 216–23: photographs by Maura McEvoy; produced by Linda O'Keeffe and Sarah Downs.

NEW ENGLAND pages 226–31: photographs by Peter Estersohn; produced by Newell Turner and Donna Paul. • 232–35: photographs by Peter Mauss; produced by Newell Turner. • 236–41: photographs by Elizabeth Heyert; produced by Linda O'Keeffe and Donna Paul. • 242–49: photographs by Antoine Bootz; produced by Donna Warner and Donna Paul.

To the architects and designers who allowed us to publish their work, to the photographers who captured it, to the homeowners who opened their doors to us, and to the city editors past and present who found and produced these locations, the editors of *Metropolitan Home* are deeply grateful.

In particular, the author extends her heartfelt thanks to four people who invested much time and faith in this project: Donna Warner, Editor in Chief, *Metropolitan Home;* Roy Finamore, Editor, Special Projects, Clarkson Potter/Publishers; Susan H. Alter, Vice President, Marketing, Hachette Filipacchi Magazines II, Inc.; and, as always, my literary agent, Dominick Abel. Rima Suqi directed the photo research; I am grateful to her.

Arlene Hirst, *Met Home*'s senior editor, design news, contributed nearly half the resources in the book, culling some from the magazine and others from her own voluminous files. The rest arrived in long lists with generous commentary from city editors Nisi Berryman, Barbara Vollmar Bohl, Diane Carroll, Pam Hait, Laura Hull, Linda Humphrey, Ellen Johnson, Donna Paul, Lisa Skolnik, and Helen Thompson. Diane Dorrans Saeks shared the resource listing in her own book, *California Design Library: Living Rooms,* as did Cara Greenberg, author of *Mid-Century Modern.* For a vast amount of research and fact-checking I am grateful to *Met Home* assistant editor Beth Mahoney, Clarkson Potter editorial assistant Chris Smith, and my former assistant, Jennifer C. Johnson. Finally, many thanks to Bo Niles, Jill Herbers, Jill Kirchner, Erica Landis, Carol Prisant, and Terry Trucco, who contributed resources or expertise to these pages.

The 39 homes in this book first appeared in the magazine in different form. All have been reported anew and rewritten—but for those originally covered by other writers, Met Home and the author gratefully acknowledge the work of Fred A. Bernstein, Jeff Book, Michael Cunningham, Edward M. Gomez, Glenn Helmers, Julie V. Iovine, Michael Lassell, Victoria Lautman, Anne Magruder, Linda O'Keeffe, Mitchell Owens, Diane Dorrans Saeks, Donna Sapolin, Liz Seymour, David Staskowski, Timothy J. Ward, and John Willoughby.

Finally, the editors are indebted to Met Home's former Editor in Chief, Dorothy Kalins, under whose stewardship many of these homes were first published.